Climb the Mountain

A Family Journey

From a Dusty Road in Afghanistan
To the Snowy Summit of Mt. Rainier

A True Story

David R. Beshears

Greybeard Publishing
Washington State

Greybeard Publishing
P.O. Box 480
McCleary, WA 98557-0480

ISBN 0-9773646-9-0

Climb the Mountain

Prolog

On Friday, October 12, 2007 at 10:00 AM, I received a phone call from a Captain Anderson from the US Army. Our son, Sergeant First Class David Michael Beshears, had been severely injured in Afghanistan.

David was part of a seven man unit training Afghani police and military. They had been pretty much on their own for their entire tour in-country. Just a few weeks earlier, they had been on a mission for which David was to earn the Bronze Star.

On this final mission, his 150th, he would earn the Purple Heart.

His unit had been traveling in two vehicles somewhere near the Pakistani border in northern Afghanistan when the forward vehicle, the one in which he had been traveling, was blown twenty feet into the air. It took 25 minutes to get him out of the Humvee. It took much longer to get a medivac to him. The team and the helicopter attempting to reach them were taking fire.

David had once said that his greatest fear was to be taken prisoner by the Taliban. Despite this, as they huddled for cover on that dusty road in a foreign land, he told his brothers-in-arms to leave him behind. However, being that these *were* his brothers-in-arms, their quick response was '*f*** you, Beshears*'.

The helicopter finally made it to them and got David out. It would be another two days before the rest of the unit made it to safety.

David was medivacked to Bagram, Afghanistan, then to Germany, and finally to Walter Reed Hospital in Washington DC. He lost consciousness somewhere en route to Bagram. Due to the concussive blast, he had suffered severe traumatic brain injury, major spinal and internal injuries.

His mom and I arrived at Walter Reed the day after David. We would spend the next six weeks there with him, most of that time in Surgical ICU. He would then spend seven months at the polytrauma unit in Palo Alto, California. There would then be months more as an inpatient in a physical therapy facility here in Washington State before he would move in with us.

This journey was documented from the very first day, beginning with daily emails that I sent to family and friends, and later through similar status updates that I entered onto a website that was written to chronicle David's Journey.

I wasn't initially aware that the daily updates that I was sending out were being forwarded on, and forwarded on, and forwarded on; not until we began receiving emails and cards from people that we didn't even know. Hundreds of people arrived at work each morning anxiously looking for the next status update in their inboxes. Church groups were holding prayer vigils. David had become a part of their lives, a part of their families. Our struggle had become their struggle.

Important Note:
The emails included throughout this book are presented unedited, shown exactly as they were originally sent out: sentence format, typos, emotional rantings and all.

The Phone Call

As a computer programmer, I'm in a position where I can telecommute from my home office on Fridays. I like working out of my office. It's quiet and I usually get more work done than on those days that I drive into Olympia.

My method of communicating with management, fellow programmers and the stakeholders of the programs that I'm developing is generally by email. I like email. I don't really like the phone.

But on this particular Friday, on October 12, 2007, at about 10:00 in the morning, I am on the phone. I'm talking with someone named Captain Anderson.

"Your son has been injured," he said. "It was a roadside bomb. I'm afraid that he's in serious condition."

When I hung up the phone, my mind and body were completely numb. I remember concentrating on each breath. My chest was shaking. It was vibrating. Something weird was happening to my heart. I don't think it was quite sure what it was supposed to do.

And yet I somehow thought to send an email to Laura, my supervisor. I was letting her know that I wasn't going to finish out the day.

My wife Sylvia made it home within an hour. She was hysterical. She began pounding her clinched fists on the kitchen counter and screaming out "No! No! No!" I tried my best to comfort her, to be strong for her. Isn't that what you're supposed to do?

I told her that from what the captain had said, that while David's injuries were serious, it sounded like he was going to be all right.

But, as we soon found out, Captain Anderson hadn't known the true severity of our son's injuries.

I would be on the phone most of that day, throughout the night, and for several days afterward. I would follow David as he moved from hospital to hospital; first to Bagram Afghanistan, then to Germany, and eventually reaching Walter Reed in Washington DC I would talk with each doctor that he was handed off to. I talked with residents and with nurses on the floor.

And I kept my supervisor informed as to what was going on. On my telecommute days, I would always let her know what I was working on, if I was going to step away from my desk, whatever. Letting her know what was happening on that Friday just seemed like the normal thing to do. As it turned out, I would continue this for months, and then for several years.

Friday, October 12, 2007
10:12AM
My son was hit with a roadside bomb.
He is in serious condition.
He has numerous injuries, legs, pelvis, abdomen.
He is in exploratory surgery for his abdomen.

Friday, October 12, 2007
1:25 PM
David is still in surgery.
All I know is that he in serious condition. I have a 1-800 number that I can call 24 hours a day.
I did find out that he is in a hospital in Bagram, Afghanistan.
The Army travel office contacted me about travel
arrangements overseas "if we are needed to be at his bedside".

Saturday, October 13, 2007
9:56 AM
David's injuries are much more severe than was first indicated.

He is in critical condition. Back fracture, spinal cord injuries, fractured pelvis, broken femur, bruised lungs, concussion, brain swelling. Infection has set in. He is under heavy sedation and is on a ventilator and is bound up in weights.

He was flown out of Afghanistan overnight and has been in surgery in Germany most of the day (it is 6:30 PM there now). If they can stabilize him enough, a team will take him to Walter Reed tomorrow (Sunday). They are concerned about his lungs during travel.

When I asked his doctor about the "life threatening" status of his injuries, her main concerns were infection from his pelvis injury, brain swelling, and clots in his lungs. These are being watched.

Monday, October 15, 2007
6:02 AM
David is at Walter Reed.

He is still in critical condition. He is on a ventilator, has a monitor in his skull to track brain swelling, and is being kept fully sedated. He is not out of the woods.

He has a crushed lumbar vertebrate, back fracture, broken femur, broken pelvis, brain concussion, bruised kidneys, bleeding around the spleen, and a lot of lesser injuries.

They tried to lower the sedatives to bring him around long enough to get info they can get only when he is conscious. However, when they did, he began involuntarily reacting to the ventilator tubes in his throat and lungs and they had to put him back under. While they were very happy at seeing such a level of response, they weren't able to get whatever info they were looking for.

They were going to send him down for CT scans overnight. They want to see if the crushed vertebrate injury also damaged his spinal cord. I will know the results this morning.

They are making arrangements to bring us to Walter Reed. We will probably be going out Wednesday night on a red-eye. I should know for sure someday today.

Tuesday, October 16, 2007
5:18 AM
We're waiting on a phone call from Walter Reed.

We're flying out tonight rather than tomorrow night. David is going into surgery today to install clot filters and surgery tomorrow for his spine.

Tuesday, October 16, 2007
8:25 AM
They are flying us out early... like early this afternoon. We're being picked up in a little while.

I know this is asking a lot, but I think that what you were putting together for my grandkids was very thoughtful (Sylvia cried. Her work had wanted to know why she didn't finish out her shift when we first got word about David). Is there any way you can send it to us?

If you can, they are putting us up at:

Courtyard by Marriott
8506 Fenton Street
Silver Spring, MD 20910

I'll let you know what happens. I'm not taking my laptop, so I won't be communicating email. I'll try and call.

During those first few days before we left for Walter Reed, Sylvia was frequently on the phone with her family. Once at Walter Reed, she would continue to talk with them regularly, but as for day by day status updates, her family would come to rely on the nightly emails that I sent out from the hotel computers.

Each evening after returning to the hotel from our day with David, I would sit at the computer kiosk in the hotel lobby and detail the events of the day. As these were going to David's grandma and grandpa, I would do my best to come up with something good that had happened. While I never hid the truth, and always gave them all the facts that I could remember, I tried my best to find something good about that day; something positive.

As I look back now, I believe those daily emails helped me get through some extraordinarily terrible times. I was forced to find a little bit of good in every day. I took that in, took it to heart, and made sure that we all saw at least some good, and thereby avoided (for the most part) letting the bad completely overwhelm us.

And when I sent this status update off to family each night, I cc'd copies to my supervisor and my IT manager. It wasn't until weeks later that I found that Laura was forwarding these updates on to dozens of other state employees who were concerned about David. Many of these folks were then forwarding them on to their coworkers, friends and family.

Walter Reed

We flew out of SeaTac airport in the early afternoon on October 16th, 2007. I don't remember too much of the flight, but I do remember coming into the airport in DC It was almost midnight and the monuments below were lit up and visible in the darkness.

If we had been on vacation, I no doubt would have been suitably impressed. As it was, what meaning they held for me was ill-omened. My son was somewhere nearby, and very bad things had happened to him.

I was surprised at how quiet the airport was. There were very few people about and what talking there was seemed hushed. We had brought only carry-on baggage, so Sylvia and I went immediately to where we were told we would be picked up. There was to be both a military and a civilian representative waiting to take us to see David and then take us on to the hotel.

No one was at the pick-up location near baggage claim. Absolutely no one; no other passengers, no airport staff, and no one waiting to meet us. That entire section of the airport was deserted.

So we waited.

After fifteen or twenty minutes I started wandering around within the terminal and on the sidewalk just outside. I finally met our guide halfway between where we were waiting and where he had been waiting. He had gotten the flight numbers wrong.

He was alone. It took another few minutes for the privately contracted SUV limo to pick us up. I never did ask about the other person that was supposed to be with him.

Being as late as it was, now well after midnight, we asked to be taken directly to the hotel. I really didn't want to go to my unconscious son's bedside in the middle of the night and see how badly he had been hurt, and then go to the hotel, lay my head on the pillow and close my eyes.

Since David had a surgery scheduled for 8:30 the next morning, we would go in at 7:00.

The drive from the airport to the hotel was surreal. Our guide made small talk, noting what the area had to offer as would any tour guide. I guess he assumed that we planned to take in the sights while we were in town.

At one point we could see the Washington and Lincoln monuments, brightly lit against the black of the night. They were wondrous sights, as they had been from the air. I tried to admire them, but they really held little interest for either of us.

Much of the drive was through residential and side streets, winding roads and very dark shadows. The driver explained that this was a faster route than taking the main streets, even late at night.

We pulled up outside the back entrance of the hotel and entered through an unattended lobby. We had to call up for the elevator that connected this lower lobby to the main lobby. We would later find that this was to be our regular access to the street. The hotel shuttle to Walter Reed would pick us up and drop us off at this back entrance. The lower lobby was never clerked.

Our guide helped us get checked into the hotel. Though our lodging was to be taken care of by the government, we did have to present a credit card for other charges that we might accrue. This would come back to bite us. The way the overnight hotel clerk incorrectly set things up, the lodging charges were held against our account each day, pending payment from the government. As we had given our check card, these lodging charges, which grew daily, were held against our checking account. Of course, we didn't realize this until Sylvia had a look at our checking account online days later.

The Marriott would face the wrath of the United States Army on this. The hotel had only recently been added to the contract to provide lodging to families of wounded soldiers. The two wars were creating a lot of wounded and current lodging hadn't been keeping up with the demand.

Still, if the Marriott expected to keep this lucrative contract, thoy had to meet all expectations. This included shuttle service to and from the hospital, clean rooms and housekeeping services, and no holding the charges on client checking and charge accounts against payments that were to be made by the government.

Our guide went with us to our room, made certain we were settled in, and had me sign a couple of documents. I think they acknowledged that he had done his job and that we were satisfied with what we had been provided.

Sylvia and I settled in for the few hours before dawn.

David's wife Semiha (Sem) had arrived at Walter Reed the day before, and she and the two kids had a room at the same hotel. Over the next day or so we would find that there were several other wounded warrior families also staying at the Marriott, as well as contract employees on assignment to Walter Reed and being billeted at the hotel.

This meant that demand for shuttle service frequently exceeded the number of available seats. In the coming weeks we would sometimes find ourselves waiting an hour or more for a ride to the hospital, or while at the hospital waiting for a ride back to the hotel. As we grew more and more exhausted, physically and mentally, day by day, this would become increasingly arduous.

The traffic between the hotel and the hospital was some of the worst that I've ever seen, and while I don't want to generalize, the drivers in that area were often some of the rudest, most inconsiderate people that I've ever come across.

But on that first morning, this very strange, very alien world barely registered on my numbed consciousness.

All we wanted to do was get to our son.

We eventually reached the Walter Reed campus gate, showed our identification and were passed through. We drove past the helipad up on the right, and were dropped off at the front doors to the hospital. In the coming weeks, our hearts would sink every time we heard a helicopter arriving. Another wounded kid was being brought in...

We walked into the hospital and lined up at the check in desk in the center of the massive front lobby. I would later see this signing in process as a rather meaningless endeavor. In a few weeks, once Sylvia and I moved to the nearby Mologne House, we would come in through an unattended side door that was accessible to anyone and was heavily used. There was also an underground route that ran from the old hospital building to the main hospital building.

For now, we followed protocol. We signed in, went to the elevators and up to the fourth floor. We walked a maze of hallways to Surgical ICU (SICU).

Stepping into our son's room sent my mind spinning. There was my boy in the hospital bed, barely recognizable and yet immediately identifiable. Ventilator tubes crawled out of his mouth, strung to his left and attached them-selves to a machine with banks of buttons, LED readings and glowing red numbers.

A wire protruded from his skull, attached to a line that ran from his brain to a machine next to his head, this also flashing a number: the pressure inside his skull.

A massive neck brace kept his head from moving. The concern wasn't that David would move on his own, but that shifting would occur when medical staff had to work with him.

Mounted on the wall behind him were green oxygen tanks and clear plastic bottles, some providing moisture to David's ventilation, some collecting moisture from the breath that the machines pushed out of his lungs.

Near the ventilation equipment was a two-foot high box that served as a thousand dollar thermometer.

On David's right was a wheeled rack apparatus containing a number of different medicines, all fed through blue plastic boxes with more flashing numbers, all sending their drugs along tubes running down to collection points surgically attached to his upper chest like Borg implants.

A weight apparatus kept David's left leg pulled toward the end of the bed.

Above his head and to one side was the monitor that displayed heart rate and blood pressure. A line ran down from this directly into his arm. The blood pressure reading was arterial, getting its measurements from directly inside the artery.

In the midst of all this technology, a twenty dollar floor fan had been placed on a metal folding chair in the corner. It struggled to keep the room from becoming too hot.

The walls on the left and right were simple curtains that separated David from other SICU patient stations. Having curtains rather than solid walls allowed staff to quickly rush from one patient to the next in the event of an emergency where every second counted.

This would happen more than a few times during our time there.

Seeing intensive care television program sets on TV in no way prepared me for that moment when I stepped into that room for the first time, and the heart-wrenching reality of SICU would be reinforced every day over the coming weeks and will stay with me forever.

David was enveloped in this grotesque nest of medical equipment, at once advanced and yet strangely primitive, all working to keep him alive. None of it was meant to make him better. Its sole purpose for being was to keep him from dying.

Beyond the near visual overload and the claustrophobic sensations was the noise. Sounds reached out from every piece of equipment; hissing, breathing, beeping, whining, whistling; all fighting for attention. Alarms sounded to alert staff that a drug was running low or that David's blood pressure was climbing again, or that his heart rate was too high or too low, or that his brain was swelling beyond acceptable limits, or that his lung expiration readings weren't what they should be.

I pushed my way through the overwhelming sights and the sounds and stood at my son's bedside. I rested a hand on his arm, reached over and cautiously touched his face. I brushed his brow, just as I had when he was little. I wanted desperately to hold him, but even if I could get through all the paraphernalia, I was afraid of doing more damage.

He was so swollen; arms, legs, torso, neck, face. Some of this was from the implosion, but most of it was from the medicines that they were giving him.

Though the doctors did not know initially, David had no shrapnel penetrate his body. The damage was from the sheer force of the concussive blast within the Humvee, and the sudden, explosive pressure of the side of the vehicle slamming into his side. His body was a deep, deep purple along the left side of his torso, from the armpit to down past his hip.

He had a deep, wide wound running down the center of his belly, three inches wide and more than a foot long. This had occurred not as a result of the blast, but later at the hospital in Bagram. This was the *exploratory surgery* that they had told me about. They had gone in looking for internal injuries. They had found some.

The wound they left behind was deep, wide, discolored, messy and ugly. It was packed now with gooey gauze that needed changing several times a day.

We spent only a little time with David before the staff had to begin making preparations to take him to surgery. They brought in portable versions of some of the monitors, reattached ventilation lines to the equipment that they mounted onto the bed, and wheeled David out. Much of this would be reattached to equipment in the operating room.

While David went off to surgery, we went in search of a waiting room. Over the next weeks, we would find several different rooms in which to wait it out, though we often ended up in the cafeteria on the third floor.

On this first morning, we found a room with couches and chairs and a flat-screen, wall-mounted television.

We were told that this would be a very long surgery, so we were surprised when after only an hour or so we were called out into the hall by the surgical team.

Thursday, October 18, 2007
(Walter Reed)
David is still in critical, and is still unconscious, but he has responded to stimuli. When his vitals show he is having difficulty, I will talk to him and we can see him calming down.

They tried to take him into surgery yesterday, but his lungs weren't providing enough oxygen, even with the ventilators. They will try again at a later date. They will be replacing his burst vertebrate with a "cage" and pin the vertebrae above and below the missing one.

We have seen movement in his upper extremities; I've seen his head move and his eyes move.

I wasn't at the hotel when the package came for the kids (I was at ICU), but the clerk was expecting the package and I guess the kids' names were on them as well, so he gave them to them when they got back to the hotel. From what my daughter-in-law says, they were a huge hit. I hope to see what they got today. Please tell everyone how much I appreciate it.

I'm sending this from the hotel kiosk email. I hope it gets to you okay.

Friday, October 19, 2007
(Walter Reed)
David went in for a surgery today. This one was to install temporary external bracing pins to the femur (upper leg), and also to work on the damaged testicle.

The external pins are to allow the doctors to remove the weighed traction. They would have liked to actually do the permanent repairs to his leg, but at the time were unsure whether he was strong enough for that surgery. They needed to remove the traction so that they can tilt his bed up. They don't like David having to lay flat all the time.

David will be able to keep both testicles. Even if he had lost one, he would have been able to produce all the testosterone he had in the past, but it's still nice he can keep them both.

Another positive that came out of this is how well he went thru the surgery. I think this will encourage the doctors to move forward with the "big" surgery, the one to go in and repair his spine. We need to realize though that even though this first surgery lasted over two hours, the next one will run 6-8 hours.

David's temperature is back to normal, and I saw that his respiration was also normal. Both of these would indicate he's coming thru the pneumonia. His blood pressure was excellent, 135 / 75. He seems very comfortable at the moment. His swelling continues to go down.

Saturday, October 20, 2007
(Walter Reed)
Little David has been moved from a traditional hospital bed to an odd contraption that holds his body, arms, legs and head in place. The bed then rolls from side to side so that fluids don't settle into one place in his lungs. The intent is to minimize the complications from pneumonia.

His lungs are actually pretty clear. His temperature rises and falls between 100 and 102. Last night, his respiration (breathing) returned to a reasonable level. We'll know more this morning.

I talked with the "infectious diseases specialist" assigned to David. She said that his lungs are looking much improved and that his white cell count is normal. A raised white cell count would be an indicator for infection. Since David's is normal, the likelihood is less that he has an infection. Because of this, she says that his temperature may be a reaction to one of the drugs they were giving him. They've taken him off the drug and are watching for signs of improvement.

Sylvia and I returned to the hotel last night with the kids to give Sem some time alone with Little David. She called later to tell us that she was talking with him and asking him to blink if he understood. She said that he blinked in reply. She asked more questions and he seemed to respond to each. We are very hopeful.

We're heading to the hospital now. Talk to you later.

Sunday, October 21, 2007
(Walter Reed)
One of the members of the neuro-surgical staff told us that the swelling of David's brain is way down from a few days ago. He said the difference is night and day. However, David is still not awake. They took him off the sedatives (still on pain meds, of course), so I'm hoping we'll see something soon.

We saw the infectious diseases specialist again. She told us that David's lungs are looking good, better all the time. And the white cell blood count is still normal.

David's temperature is averaging between 99 and 100.

He will be on the ventilator until he is fully conscious and fully aware. This is standard procedure. They have been making adjustments to the levels (pressure and oxygen) as his lung condition fluctuates. Two things in particular I have noticed. The first is what is called the PEEP, which has to do with the amount of pressure applied that opens areas of the lungs. Lower number indicates his lungs are doing more on their own. They've lowered the number over the last few days from 18 to 10. This is good. The second item is the percent oxygen. The doctors wanted to be able to drop this number to 40% and have his lungs continue maintain oxygen between 96 and 100. They were able to do this yesterday. So, he's doing good there.

The head neurosurgeon is planning to get Little David in for his back surgery on Tuesday. This is a really good sign, because he will not do the surgery until he thinks David is healthy enough for it.

The only other surgery that David will need is the final work on his leg. He currently has the temporary external bracing and pins holding his femur together (apparatus looks scary, but it's doing the job). They will be replacing this with permanent internal rods later).

Improvements continue. Good news every day. We are all feeling very positive about what we're seeing and hearing.

As his Dad, I would like to see him open his eyes and show more positive awareness, but he has been under varying levels of heavy sedation since this all happened. He has been off them since yesterday, but his body is still under the influence of a week's worth of medication and the trauma that he has suffered. I am probably expecting too much too soon. Nonetheless, I will be asking the neurosurgeon tomorrow what he would normally expect to see under these conditions.

We should know more about the plans for Tuesday's surgery sometime tomorrow.

**Monday, October 22, 2007
(Walter Reed)**
Well, it looks like the doctors won't be able to do the surgery tomorrow (Tuesday) the way they had planned. This is just precautionary, but it is certainly frustrating for us.

Little David's ICP (pressure from brain swelling) has crept back up a little, and the doctors are concerned that moving him around during surgery would cause it to rise further.

They believe that the raised ICP is due to the rolling of the bed (that they brought in to prevent fluid settling in his lungs), and is not due specifically to his injuries. His swelling is still way, way down from what it was a few days ago.

A specialist (yes, another one) is coming in to determine which bed would be best for David. In the meantime, they have stopped the rolling, and we are already seeing the ICP number drop. Right now it is fluctuating between 18 and 21. This is good. One of the nursing staff had previously told us that they want the ICP at 21 or lower.

They are also going to take the ventilator and feeding tubes from his mouth and send the ventilator thru a trach tube (a hole in his throat) and the feeding tube thru his abdomen. This will make David much more comfortable. The more comfortable he is, the better his vitals.

David's digestive system appears to be working just fine (this is just what it sounds like). This says a lot about his overall health. Odd, the things we cheer about.

We should be able to talk with the neurosurgeon tomorrow. We'll have a better idea of what the plans are after that.

His blood pressure, respiratory, heart rate and temperature are all good. He's been given a new sedative, and this is also making him more comfortable. His nurse told me that one side effect is short term memory loss. He doesn't want David to remember any of the pain. Of course, this also means that he won't be regaining consciousness any time soon.

If you have any questions, don't be afraid to send them to me. I check this email address every day.

Sylvia and I would see someone with no legs sitting and talking with his family, or someone with artificial legs strapped on and walking (or running) along the sidewalk, wearing shorts so that he could display his shiny new cyborg legs, and I would find myself thinking how lucky he was, how lucky his family was.

Everything that poor kid had gone through, *would* go through in his life, and I was envious. I didn't like that I felt that way, but I couldn't help it. I would have traded my kid's legs away in a second to have him conscious and talking to me.

We were becoming jaded to the sights and sounds around us. We found ourselves walking past kids in wheelchairs, missing body parts, and not thinking twice about it.

It wasn't that I was wallowing in self-pity. I'm not even sure that I believed yet that it was real. I walked around in a fuzzy daze. I was still numb to it all. And I was angry.

In spite of that, we never lashed out at the staff. I knew that it wasn't their fault. Besides, at the time they were taking enough crap from several of the families of the other wounded.

Just as we had quickly become jaded to the sights and sounds of the world of Walter Reed, so it seems that this bizarre setting was itself jaded to this horrible thing that had happened to David. I continually wanted to scream out against this awful place, to cry out for somebody to do something, for somebody to fix this and make him okay.

Can't you see what's happened to my son? Make my boy better, goddamn it. Fix him.

But there were so many Davids in their world. True, the vast majority of the wounded warriors at Walter Reed were dealing with the loss of limbs, where my son and just a handful of others (whom we would get to know) were dealing with severe brain trauma, but they were no less deserving of attention than David.

But that was the world of Walter Reed; not <u>my</u> world. In <u>my</u> world, my boy wouldn't wake up. In my world, I wanted everyone to stop whatever else they were doing and pay attention to my boy. I wanted them to wake my boy up. I wanted to grab every doctor that walked passed my boy's room by his wrinkled white collar and drag his ass over to David's bed and make him fix my son.

Tuesday, October 23, 2007
(Walter Reed)
Here's the latest...

David is still pretty much out of it, under sedation, but his vitals all look excellent but for a bit of a fever.

He is much more comfortable in his new bed, and they have his head raised. Docs are happy about that.

The doctors did what one of them called a "brain doppler" on him. This gave them a picture of the blood flow thru-out his brain. Results were great. Blood is flowing normally thru all parts of his brain.

The doctors also did another CT Scan on David's brain, and the results of this one are better than the one yesterday, which was better than the one before that. The neuro-surgical staff is very pleased with the way he continues to improve.

They lowered David's sedatives a couple of hours ago in order to do a stimuli test on him. This is where they poke pins and pinch fingers. They were ecstatic when he opened his eyes to one of the pinchings. Then they sent him back under the sedatives.

The neuro-surgical staff is waiting for the ICU staff to tell them that David's lungs are strong enough before going in and doing the spinal surgery. ICU is still providing a significant portion of the oxygen for David, and while David initiates each breath, the ventilator takes care of 40% of the oxygen and handles the exhales.

David looks more comfortable now than I've seen him since we've been here. His vitals look better than I've seen them since we've been here. As soon as his lungs are strong enough, he'll get the spinal surgery taken care of, after which they will be able to roll him from side to side, which will make all his other healing processes go more smoothly.

For those who asked, our address here at the hotel:

Courtyard by Marriott
8506 Fenton St.
Silver Spring, MD 20910
telephone: 301.589.4899
room: 502

Talk to you later.

As Sylvia and I were "on orders", we were required to check in with military officials each week. They set up a table in the lobby of the Mologne House, a hotel on the hospital campus and very near the hospital itself. They held weekly meetings in one of the conference rooms directly off the lobby, during which new arrivals would receive an orientation from all the different organizations that were providing support. The meetings also gave those who have been around a while a chance to ask questions about issues they might have come across.

The first meeting was informative and we gathered together a lot names and brochures and binders full of info. We got very little from the second meeting, and since follow-up meetings were voluntary from that point on we would only drop in each week to sign in and make our presence known.

We were horrified to find that there were families of wounded soldiers that, once arriving on orders, collected their per diem and then went on vacation. This explained the ICU patients that we saw day in and day out that never seemed to have visitors.

The support environment encouraged families to step away from it now and then, for your own health and well being, but some of these families coming in simply collected the money and vanished, leaving their wounded soldiers to lay there all alone. The thought of it still upsets me.

Wednesday, October 24, 2007
(Walter Reed)
It's all good news today.

David opened his eyes today. He's off sedation, is now only on pain medication. He doesn't yet respond to direct commands (meaning he doesn't squeeze your hand when you tell him to), but he will open his eyes when you speak to him, when the doctors pinch him or poke him.

I was holding his hand when the nurse was trying to find a place to insert an IV stint and he squeezed my hand in response to the pain of the needle. Sounds bad, but it is great.

He doesn't yet move his eyes to your movement. He won't yet look directly at you.

I am continually telling him where he is, that he is safe, that he has injuries but is getting better. Once, not long after telling him where he was, I asked him if he remembered that he is at Walter Reed. He blinked five or six times rapidly. It didn't look involuntary. It looked like he was trying to answer me.

More good news:

The doctors have scheduled his neuro surgery (spine) for Friday and his orthopedic surgery (femur) for Monday. They wouldn't be doing this if they didn't think he was ready.

The nurse told us that since David has been so responsive today, so soon after coming out of the sedation and opening his eyes, that he believes David will be responding to commands in the next day or two.

Thursday, October 25, 2007
(Walter Reed)
The doctors continue to adjust David's ventilator as he takes on more of the work of breathing. This includes the level of oxygen, the pressure, etc. The ventilator is now in "assist" mode rather than "control" mode.

David was calm and resting all day today (thursday). If the vitals are any indicator, he was sleeping. He only opened his eyes a few times, and I would speak calmly to him and he would go right back to sleep.

His fluid swelling (puffy body) continues to go down. He looks almost normal in that respect.

The urologist came in to look at his testicles again. He took one look and told me we can take this off our list of concerns.

The neurologist said that the spinal surgery is set for Monday and not Friday. He said he doesn't know what happened, but that despite what was on the books, he had never intended on doing the surgery on Friday. So... Monday it is.

Another set of doctors are going to be putting what is called a "peg" into David's abdomen and moving the feeding tube from his throat to this peg. This is set for tomorrow (Friday) morning.

Friday, October 26, 2007
(Walter Reed)
The doctors put the "peg" in today. This is used to connect the feeding tube at his abdomen rather than his stomach. It went real well.

They have set the ventilator to a "spontaneous" mode, and it has been going well for a couple of hours now. This is where the ventilator provides air but David does all the actual work. So far, so good.

David was having a bit of a spell when we went into his room this morning. He seemed quite agitated, and his numbers were bouncing around. When I looked into his eyes to calm him down, I could see real emotion there. This was a first. It may have been a bit scary for us to go thru (scarier for him), but it is good news. This was the most aware I've seen him.

On several occasions this afternoon, David came out of his "sleepful" state, and his numbers would creep up a few points. Each time I talked to him, his numbers subsided. Finally, when he was asleep and I let go of his hand and started to back away, he came out of it again and the numbers went back up. I took his hand and he went back to sleep. For me, this is a clear sign that he is aware of what is going on around him (Sylvia and I stayed until we were sure he was going to stay asleep. Sem and Kevin came in to sit with him).

The spinal surgery is still set for Monday. The trach surgery is set for that same time. This will allow the ventilator tubes to be

taken out of his throat, connected at his trach. If David is fully
aware and conscious by that time, then the ventilator (and the
trach surgery) won't be necessary.

Saturday, October 27, 2007
(Walter Reed)
Pretty quiet today.

The swelling continues to go down. His feet and ankles are still
puffy, his stomach looks like a beer belly, but overall he looks
very good.

Twice today his eyes drifted to me. I don't know if he was
actually trying to look at me, but it appeared that way.

His ventilator continues to be on "spontaneous" mode, which
means that David is doing the work and the ventilator is simply
providing the air and is there if needed.

While I would have liked for David to have gone into surgery
before now, he is getting stronger every day and he will be
better prepared for the surgery when it comes.

Monday, October 29, 2007
(Walter Reed)
Little David spent ten hours in surgery yesterday. The doctors
had planned to perform the operation in two stages, but only
managed to get thru stage one before they called a halt. They
want to give his lungs time to recover.

The first stage went very well. The doctors went in thru the
front, cleaned out all the bone fragments (from the burst
vertebrate) and made repairs. Once this was done, they
installed the "cage" and some other hardware to replace the
vertebrate.

The purpose of the second stage, when they go back in, will be
to add support to what they installed in stage one. They will be
going in thru the back for this one. No date/time set for it.
Whenever David is strong enough.

The stage one work will allow David to sit up a bit more, which will allow his lungs to get stronger. Almost as importantly, he can begin the healing process.

Big news... The doctors didn't see any permanent damage to his spinal cord while they were working on him.

Also, we think we may have seen the first indication of David responding to a direct command. Prior to going into surgery, the nurse was asking him to perform simple tasks. In most cases, there was nothing, but when he asked David to move his right foot, we saw one toe move. What a sight that was.

He is still very responsive to external stimuli, sounds and touch.

I'm sending this out Tuesday morning (eastern time). We got back to the hotel so late last night that I was too beat to go to the computer.

While we don't yet know when David is set for the second stage of the spinal surgery, we were told that he is going in for the "ortho" surgery (leg and pelvis) on Friday.

Tuesday, October 30, 2007
(Walter Reed)
Well... today's news isn't quite as good as yesterday's...

David's fever is back up, continues to slide up and down between 101 and 103. The doctors are going to draw some spinal fluid and test it to see if there may be a cause in there somewhere.

Also, David is still not responding to direct commands when doctors try to get him to wiggle his toes or squeeze a hand. However, he was very lethargic today following the ten hours in surgery yesterday. While we might have expected to see something positive when they lowered his pain meds for the test, he was clearly slower and less aware than in past days. In addition, when I asked him to blink twice for me earlier today, he did, though because it took him five seconds to do so, the nurse was reluctant to log it as a positive response. It may not have been in direct response to me, but David almost never blinks (kind of eerie). He hadn't blinked for some time prior and didn't blink for a long time after the two blinks.

And... there was that toe that he moved yesterday...

Sem saw David move his eyes in her direction when she was talking to him and said it wasn't the blank stare we have been seeing. That would be great news. Maybe we'll see more of that tomorrow.

But for the fever, David's vitals are good, and his lungs continue to get stronger.

We're all pretty tired here... getting a bit worn down. Sylvia and I brought the kids back to the hotel a little early today, giving Sem some quiet time with David.

Wednesday, October 31, 2007
(Walter Reed)
Today didn't start out too well, but it ended on a much higher note.

When we first went in to see David this morning (went in a few hours later than usual), we were told that he had a quiet night, but again there was no response to direct commands. We didn't want to hear that, and we weren't dealing with it very well.

After a few minutes, we had a real shocker.

I was standing on one side of David's bed, Sem was standing on the other. I talked to David, the way I always do, and his eyes tracked to me. I cried. Sylvia, standing at the foot of the bed, burst into tears. Sem talked to David, and his eyes tracked to the other side and he looked at her.

His nurse for the day was overjoyed. She talked to David, and was quite excited. She hurried out to her station and I could hear her making comments like: "he's tracking their movement, he's tracking their movement!"

Nurses who have been working with David over the past weeks came in, hugging Sylvia and smiling and saying how wonderful this was.

It wasn't much, but it was everything. In later attempts, David sometimes had trouble, sometimes you could see the muscles trying to work. He managed some more eye movement, both to Sem and to me. He looked at his son, and that was great.

The nurses want us to continue to work with him, and to encourage him to squeeze our fingers on command. The next big step.

The physical therapists and occupational therapists have given us exercises for him (simple things to loosen tightened muscles, etc).

Other stuff:

The doctors tested David's spinal fluid and he does not have meningitis. That's a relief. This had been a concern.

Doctors found that he has an infection in his pancreas. This is most likely the source of his ongoing fever. At least we know, and now they can treat the cause and not just the symptoms.

David goes in for the second half of his spinal surgery tomorrow (Thursday). The first stage had been to clean out all the bone fragments and install the "cage". The second stage will be to put in the pins and rods to fuse the spine.

David will finally have his broken femur and pelvis taken care of on Friday. Up to now he's had the external pins and bracing (an ugly contraption).

We have been told that if all goes well and once David recovers from the surgeries, he will be transferred to a facility that specializes in spinal injury and brain trauma recovery. They had talked about Tampa, but we have requested Palo Alto, CA. David, Sem and the kids would be much nearer family support there. We should know in a few days. David will likely go out in a couple of weeks.

Sylvia and I plan to leave for home when David is shipped out, then follow him to Palo Alto after we spend a few days taking care of things at home. All of this depends on how things go over the next days.

Thursday, November 01, 2007
(Walter Reed)
The doctors didn't do his neuro surgery (final work on spinal) today. The head neurosurgeon had to go to Bethesda. I'm not sure when the surgery will be.

The orthopedic surgeons don't want to do the ortho surgery (pelvis and femur) until after the neuro has been done, so David won't have that surgery tomorrow, as had been scheduled.

He did have the trach this afternoon. Took a couple of hours. The ventilator has been taken from his mouth and is now connected at his throat. He should be much more comfortable now.

The doctors are still trying to locate the cause for his fever. It wasn't the pancreas, though this has become inflamed. When we left David this evening, his temperature was down to 99. He's been down to normal before. We're hoping this one holds.

We didn't see much in the way of response to direct commands today. The doctors are going to back off the pain medication over the next couple of days, so we're hoping to see some improvement soon.

Friday, November 02, 2007
(Walter Reed)
A bit quiet today, but there were a couple of items of note...

The doctors removed the ventilator from David's trach and hooked up oxygen and humidifier to the trach. David is breathing completely on his own, enriched oxygen. He gets a bit uncomfortable now and then, and the nurse says it will take David a couple of days to get used to it. After all, he was on a ventilator for almost three weeks.

The doctors took David off the pain medication at 8:00 AM this morning. They want to clean the meds out of his system in order to determine if this is why he isn't more responsive.

Speaking of responsive... David was very quiet day, more so than in recent days. He appears to be tired and sleeping. Several doctors agree with this. He has spent a long time on the pain meds, and the rest you get from this isn't the same as sleep. Now that he's off them, he's sleeping. Another doctor pointed out that being completely off the ventilator can make you very tired. So... he's sleeping and doesn't want to be bothered.

Doctors are feeding David thru an IV in order to bypass the digestive system. He has an inflamed pancreas, and the treatment is to give it nothing to do.

Neuro is doing the second surgery on Monday.

That's it for now...

It had been about three weeks since we had arrived in DC Back and forth, every day, hotel to hospital in the morning, back to the hotel at night.

Sem was going to be leaving with the kids and heading back to Oklahoma soon, where they were stationed and still had the house. David and Sem's daughter Ashley had a heart condition and a procedure had been on the schedule for some time. The date was coming up. In spite of the circumstances, this wasn't something to be put off.

Sylvia and I would of course be staying with David. The hope was that we would all be meeting up in California before too long.

That was still very much up in the air, and much of it depended on whom you talked to. Some said that he wasn't going anywhere, others said that it shouldn't be too long at all.

All agreed that David had to meet certain criteria, pass certain milestones, before anything could happen.

I was beginning to see that some of the medical staff had expected certain things to have happened by now and were at somewhat of a loss as to why they hadn't. They didn't say anything specific to me, but I could see that he wasn't coming out of it as they had hoped. I found myself pointing out to them every little positive thing that I saw and was actually pushing them to take what we were getting and to run with it.

I was getting more and more of those 'oh, you poor deluded dad' looks. Really pissed me off.

Sunday, November 04, 2007
(Walter Reed)
There was a big change in David today (Sunday). He had been very unresponsive over the past few days, and we had been growing more and more concerned. Today, however, he was very aware of sights and sounds around him, and is again opening his eyes at the calling if his name or a sharp sound in the room. We were very glad to see that.

He is back to breathing on his own with an oxygen tube resting next to his trach. This time, he is breathing easy. When they took him off the ventilator before, he had a hard time adjusting. Somewhere along the line, someone put him back on the ventilator. When the head doctor saw it, he firmly stated "get him off that thing".

Once David had the trach done and the tubes removed from his mouth, we had our first look in his mouth. We saw that his front teeth had been... moved. It looked pretty bad. The two front teeth were pushed up and spread apart. Sem and I asked to have someone look at it. I'm afraid they had to pull the teeth. Whatever damage had been done initially by the blast was made worse by three weeks of having the teeth pressed against the tubes. There wasn't much holding them in place. We're told he can have implants put in. He's not going to be happy about this. He was always a bit obsessive about taking care of his teeth. I did get a chance to look closely in his mouth and was able to see that the other teeth look like they're in good shape.

Anyway... like I said, David looks pretty good today. He's breathing good and he seems more aware than he has in days. They have him on low dose of pain meds, and this may be better than when they took him off it all together. With no pain meds at all, I think we was so focused on the pain that he ignored us. Today, there were a couple of times I think he might have actually responded to commands, but I'm just not sure.

I came back to the hotel early today, with Sem and the kids. They had to head out to the airport. With Ashley's heart procedure coming up, they had to get home. Sylvia and I will be hanging on here and hopefully see David off to Palo Alto soon. We're not sure how long before that happens. The ICU team is saying that David's not going anywhere. Others are saying it's only a matter of a couple weeks. I think we'll know more by the middle of next week.

One other item... because David had grown so quiet for several days after that great morning when he had been tracking our movement with his eyes, I voiced my concern to the staff. They agreed to order another CT scan of his brain. The results showed there had been no change. This is good, since previous scans showed his brain to be doing well. Some of the staff continue to say that David may just be overly tired from coming off the ventilator and no longer having it as a crutch to fall back on whenever he wants to. To be honest, some others aren't quite as optimistic. The neuro staff continue to be very positive.

Monday, November 05, 2007
(Walter Reed)
David had his second spinal surgery today. The surgeon said
there were no surprises and that it went very well. His spine
can now begin the healing process.

We're waiting to hear from the ortho team about when they
want to do the surgery on his femur and pelvis. They had been
waiting for neuro to finish, so I'm hoping David's final surgery
will be in the next day or two.

David was wide awake when we went to see him before he
went into surgery this morning. We got to his room about 7:10
and were able to spend 20 minutes with him. He didn't respond
to direct commands but he seemed as aware of his
surroundings (response to stimuli) as we've seen him.

I sat with him for several hours following his surgery, watched
as he slowly came around, began to open his eyes, respond to
sounds around him, respond to bumps of the bed. I take this all
as very positive. His mind is definitely working and taking in the
outside world.

One of the doctors on general staff told me that David is
responding to the antibiotics they are giving him for his
infection and the bacteria in his blood. He said they may never
know the source, but his fever and the level of infection and
bacteria continue to trend downward, with occasional spikes.

Sylvia and I were talking to one of our favorite nurses today,
and she says that she sees no reason why David couldn't be
transferred to Palo Alto once ortho completes the surgery on
his leg and pelvis. The only med he's on now is the pain med,
and he is now only on the ventilator during and immediately
after surgeries. So who knows, ortho does their thing, then give
ICU a few more days to monitor David's recovery from both the
neuro and ortho surgeries, and we might just be outta here.
Man, I hope so...

From what Sylvia and I saw with Little David today, I really think
we might see even more response from him tomorrow. We

know we'll have more setbacks, but I believe we'll begin seeing more and more forward progress now.

We're back in the hotel this afternoon, came in a couple of minutes ago (it's about 2:40 our time). Sylvia is still a bit sick, but getting better. I wasn't too well for a few days last week, but I'm much better now. We're going to rest this afternoon while David sleeps.

Sylvia got pretty sick with some flu bug, and she had to stay off the SICU floor for a while. I continued seeing David alone for a couple of days while we were still staying at the Marriott, and a few more once we moved to the Mologne House. The medical staff said that David was safe enough, what with all the medications he was on... they were more concerned about the staff.

Besides, Sylvia and I were both so run down by now that if she expected to get better, she needed to rest.

We had begun asking about the possibility of moving over the Mologne House, and in the end it was a simple matter of getting on the waiting list. After that, it only took a couple of days. I was to call each day around noon. On the second or third day, they told me they had a room for us.

The move to the Mologne House really helped us both. We no longer had to make that grinding commute each morning and each night, since it was only a five minute walk to the hospital.

This also meant that I could leave the hospital at noon and head back to the Mologne House and have lunch there. Stepping away at midday did amazing things for my wellbeing.

Tuesday, November 06, 2007
(Walter Reed)

David was pretty quiet today, much as he was the day after his last surgery, but did appear to be very aware of activity around him. Once, his nurse came in and called out "hello, David!" and startled David so much I thought he was going to jump out of the bed.

This afternoon, the neuro surgical team went back in for a minor adjustment to one of the screws they put in yesterday. Once he was prepped and then put under, it only took them twenty minutes and it went fine. But now he won't be awake for few hours.

The doctors told me that the inflamed pancreas is getting better with the treatment. They are going to slowly begin feeding him through the tube that is connected to the peg in his stomach. He has been on IV feed for several days.

The ICU medical team makes rounds to each patient each day, and when they come to stand outside David's area, I always stand in and integrate myself into the discussion. Don't know if they all like it or not, but they talk to me and even ask me questions about my observations. By now I think I could pass for a TV doctor. During today's discussion they commented that David will soon be able to transition from "Critical to Rehab". Whatever David's future might be, at least they are now officially talking beyond ICU.

One of David's ICU nurses told us that she has already requested that she be the ICU nurse to accompany David to Palo Alto.

No word on exactly when ortho plans on doing their thing (final surgery), beyond vague references to "end of the week". This last surgery needs to happen before the transition that ICU is talking about can take place.

Thursday, November 08, 2007
(Walter Reed)
I'm sending this out thursday morning before I go up to see David.

We were moving from the Marriott to the Mologne House yesterday afternoon. We are now within walking distance of the hospital. If I go out the back, I can get to David's room in about five minutes.

The phone number for our room is: 202.577.0009

David can't seem to lose the fever. When I left him last night, it had gone down to 99.9, but it had been as high as 102 yesterday. I haven't checked yet this morning.

I saw David grimace yesterday. It happened when his heart rate went up and he clinched his hands, so I know it was because he was in pain. I told the nurse we had a soldier in pain over here, and he came and gave him a booster on his pain meds. I don't like that he was in pain, but this was the first time I've seen him make so dramatic a facial expression. Oh... and I went to the doctor on the floor and told him about David's pain and continued high heart rate. He made adjustments to his pain medication regimen.

I heard the doctors again mention that they were working to "Palo Alto" David. I asked one doctor what he thought the timeline might be, and he said that the only outstanding issues before transitioning him were the fever/infection and the remaining work that ortho needs to do on his leg. He told me it might be as early as the middle of next week, but not to hold him to that. So I'm thinking we can hope for the middle of next week, but not expect anything before the end of next week.

I'm heading over to the hospital right now. I will update later today (Thursday).

Thursday, November 08, 2007
Afternoon
(Walter Reed)

Now that we're staying in the Mologne House, I can come down for lunch and check my email from my room.

I wanted to let you know what news I have from this morning...

Last evening and this morning, David's heart rate continued to be up. When I went in this morning, it was still up in the 120s, though this is down from last night. I sat and talked quietly to him, like I do, let him know I was there and that I was watching out for him. He relaxed and his heart rate went down about 20 points. It usually seems to help.

The doctors, seeing this, began discussing how the heart rate, an indicator of pain, may also be indicating anxiety. Gee... big news. They told us the first day that we should continue reassuring David that he is safe, that he is at Walter Reed, that he is surrounded by family.

At any rate, they are going to provide medication for anxiety.

After the doctors moved on in their rounds, I continued sitting with David. I was able to get his heart rate to about 110. Then, during one of the moments when he opened his eyes, I stood slightly to one side and told him to look over at me. His eyes began moving in shaky jerks and his eyelids fluttered oddly as though he was trying to focus. He looked at me. After about 5 seconds, he moved his eyes back and closed them. As he did, his heart rate went down to 95.

I "hissed" for the nurse to get in here, told him what had happened. I told him that whatever changes he had made to the meds must be working. He said it wasn't the meds. He said that David had seen his Dad's face and recognized it, heard Dad's voice and felt Dad holding his hand. He feels safe now.

Cool.

David has been sleeping ever since. The best sleep he's had in three weeks. And his heart rate is staying down, at least for now.

The ortho team asked for xrays of David's leg this morning, but as yet no word on when they intend to fix his leg. During morning rounds, one of the head doctors asked the intern making the report what he had been told from ortho. When the intern said they hadn't told him anything, the doctor told him to "get on the phone, tell ortho to give you an answer. Tell them they are holding up this soldier going to rehab. Tell them that Mom and Dad want to take their boy home".

I bet we have an answer this afternoon.

I do know that ICU has begun coordinating David's planned move to Palo Alto. They have been talking about getting a plane and discussing the staff that would go down with him.

David is still fighting some infection, and his temperature fluctuates from near normal up to 102.

They have taken David off the IV feed and are feeding him through the peg in his abdomen.

David's breathing is very good. He is breathing through the trach in his neck, seems comfortable. They still have to suction him a couple of times a day. This is his least favorite thing in the entire world.

A new physical therapist came by and gave me a full set of exercises for David. Some David was okay with, some he wasn't too happy about.

Enough for now. I'm walking back over to the hospital...

Friday, November 09, 2007
(Walter Reed)
Laura & Gary,

Please pass along my thanks to everyone for all the support. We get cards every day wishing David well and offering prayers.

The front desk at the Marriott said they've never seen anything like it. Dozens and dozens of cards. Now that we've moved over to the Mologne House, the Marriott shuttle driver was kind enough to bring the latest batch to us. I had asked the Marriott to forward mail here, but the driver said he was happy to bring them over.

Not sure how much longer we'll be here before heading to Palo Alto. I'm guessing a week or week and a half. Sylvia and I will go back home first to take care of everything that we left hanging there.

Again, tell everyone how much we appreciate their kind words,

David

Friday, November 09, 2007
Afternoon
(Walter Reed)
All good news this friday midday.

When I went in first thing this morning, Little David was very alert, and appeared comfortable. He is very responsive to everything going on around him. He looks really, really good.

A few minutes later, I asked David to look over at me, and he did. His eyes tracked over and he looked directly at me; clear, sharp eyes.

When the nurse went to his other side and asked him to look over at her, he unfortunately wouldn't take his eyes off me. One of the other staff said that David knew who he was looking at and didn't want to look away. I'll take that, at least for now.

Later, physical therapy was working on him. The therapist would ask David to push back, to blink, to move an arm, and on several occasions the therapist would tell me that David was responding to his direct commands.

Ortho says they're not going to do the surgery to put the rod into his leg. They say that David's femur is healing fine with the external rods and pins. Of course, this means that at some point somebody is going to have to go in and take out that apparatus.

David's fever is down, white count is normal, heart rate continues to look good. ICU says that the only thing stopping David from going to Palo Alto is mountains of paperwork. I guess Palo Alto hasn't yet given the final go-ahead. I'm not sure what's going on there.

One of the doctors told me that David can leave ICU tomorrow. If Palo Alto isn't ready for him, he will probably be moved to "step down", which is actually some room upstairs. I hear it's more comfortable. That would be great. I've been standing next to David's bed, or sitting in a folding chair, surrounded by critical care equipment, for over three weeks.

I'm going to have some lunch now and then head back to David's room.

It was during the second week in November that the weather at Walter Reed really started turning cold. I had to brace myself before setting out on that walk between the Mologne House and the hospital. I was initially on my own, since it was at the time of the move from the hotel that Sylvia was so sick, and then later we would strike out together and take that back route.

Between the Mologne House and the hospital, along a back walkway, was an old, large building that had been boarded up. The sidewalk ran right past the front plaza of the abandoned structure. It had the look of one of those scary old hospitals that you see in horror B movies. A number of upper floor windows were open, bent blinds hanging out.

Signs on the door warned of asbestos. A plaque on a pedestal outside mentioned something about a medical research facility.

I'll always remember walking past the lonely old place on those cold, gray, bitter November mornings, hunched over and wrapped up in my coat against freezing wind.

Saturday, November 10, 2007
(Walter Reed)
David continues to be alert, quite aware of his surroundings.

He looked over at me a number of times when I asked him to yesterday evening and this morning (since yesterday's email). He did the same once for one of the doctors. This is Sylvia's first day back to see him after three days away. David moved his eyes and looked at Sylvia once this morning.

There were a few minutes this morning when I had him blinking, closing his eyes, opening his eyes.

He continues to respond well to my voice. Our goal now is have him respond to our commands consistently, every time.

Sunday, November 11, 2007
(Walter Reed)
David has been more responsive to direct commands in past
days than he was today, but there is very good news about his
attention to things going on around him.

I watched as David moved his eyes from one thing to another
around the room. He was focusing on different things that
caught his attention. This is new and very positive. He hadn't
done this before today.

A little later, I was sitting beside David's bed and we were
watching the football game (Redskins/Eagles) on the television.
David was looking at the screen. When the doctor came and
stood in the doorway (to one side of the tv), I stood and walked
over to talk with him. The doctor smiled broadly and said that
he saw that David had been watching the television, but had
turned his eyes to look at me as I walked over.

This is very, very good.

David did have a bit of a rough afternoon. The doctors are
trying to switch him from the IV pain meds to oral medication,
meaning thru his feeding tube. He didn't handle the transition
too well, and had an uncomfortable couple of hours until they
got the IV pain meds back into him.

The doctors believe that even though his bowels are working
well, they may not have fully absorbed the morphine. They are
going to continue with both types and slowly wean him off the
IV pain meds as the oral meds begin to work. David needs to be
off the IV meds before he can go to Palo Alto.

David is being moved from the Intensive Care Unit to the
Intermediate Care Unit this evening. He will still be under
continual observation, will have many of the same medical
staff, but he no longer needs the heavy duty stuff of ICU. He
will still be hooked up to all the same monitors, but his vitals
will be logged in every two hours instead of every hour. The
ward he's going to is smaller and quieter than where he is now.

That's it for now.

David made the move from Surgical ICU (SICU) to Intermediate ICU (IICU) Sunday night, November 11th, almost a month to the day after he was injured. IICU was supposed to provide almost the same attention and observation as SICU, but with a little less of the intensive monitoring.

SICU was careful about moving their patients over too soon. They had seen them come right back all too often, and it's not good for the patient, the family, or the staff to have someone bounced back and forth.

As it would turn out, he would only be in IICU for two nights. He wouldn't be going back to SICU, but rather continue to move 'up and out'.

This would be a good thing, for more reasons than one.

We found out that on David's second night in the IICU ward, not long after we left him in the care of the staff and returned to the Mologne House, that the nursing staff left the unit.

It seemed that Bruce Springsteen had shown up on the general ward up on the 5th floor and the staff wanted to see him.

So they left David alone. I about freaked. David needed to be under constant observation. That was why he was where he was. Even after he would make the move up to the 5th floor, he would be assigned a room in direct line of sight to the nursing station and would have someone assigned to sit outside his door twenty four hours a day.

To leave him alone so they could pop upstairs to catch a glimpse of Bruce Springsteen was criminal.

I didn't put this little tidbit into the status updates at the time because I didn't want to frighten Sem or David's grandparents. There was enough going on without throwing in medical abandonment. The fact that David was moving out of SICU was supposed to be good news.

An interesting thing about the general ward that Springsteen visited was that since the public had easier access to this floor than to any of the ICU wards, there were a lot of visitors that were unknown to the patients who were staying there. Most were well-meaning people, many representing groups and clubs from around the country that were looking for a way to help out. People would drop by with donations of books and magazines, phone cards, caps and shirts. Yes, some were celebrities, some were politicians.

Once we made the move up to the ward, David had lots of such visitors. Though he was still in a relative vegetative state, he didn't really look like it. People would drop in and try to talk to him, and when they would get no response they would turn to me and give me an odd look. When I would point out that David wasn't all the way back to us just yet, in as kind a way as I could, most would get a stricken look on their faces and back out of the uncomfortable situation as quickly as possible.

A few though, usually representatives from one military organization or another, would ask me for permission to approach my son. They would shake hands with David or place a hand on his shoulder, and tell him how honored they were to be in the presence of a hero who had sacrificed so much.

The secretary of one of the highest ranking politicians in Washington DC at the time came into the room one day. She said that this politician was out in the hall and would like to come in to say hello to David. I declined. It was a gut reaction. I wasn't ready to deal with politicians. Too many were, well... I still don't want to go there.

Monday, November 12, 2007
(Walter Reed)
David made the move over to the intermediate care ward last night. The night was fairly quiet.

They are slowly lowering the IV pain med while maintaining the oral pain med (thru his stomach peg). David is managing well so far.

This morning, David's nurse had him rolled onto his side and was using the stethoscope to listen to his lungs. She asked David to take a deep breath, and he did. She got really excited. Then, each time she moved the stethoscope, David took another deep breath.

I had been standing outside the curtain, but when I heard the nurse talking to David, telling him how great he was doing, I of course stepped back in to ask if he had actually been doing what she told him to. She was almost bubbly, nodding excitedly. We almost high-fived each other.

David's doctors are talking about moving David up to the general ward, completely out of ICU, within the next day or so. This is the final step to getting him to Palo Alto.

Tuesday, November 13, 2007
(Walter Reed)
Well, tuesday evening about 6:15. We just got back from the hospital.

David wasn't very responsive to us today, though he continues to react to sounds and other external stimuli. I believe some of his lack of response may be due to the fact that the doctors completed moving David off the IV pain meds last night. Since then, he has been on the oral morphine, given to him thru his feeding tube. He is given a dose every four hours. I don't think he's completely comfortable with this just yet, but if he's going to be able to make the move to Palo Alto, this has to happen.

David is moving up to general ward tonight, after only one day in the Intermediate Care Unit. This is another requirement of Palo Alto. He has to be stable outside of an ICU environment. The fact that the medical staff thinks he's ready is good news.

Because of David's status as a brain trauma patient, he is being assigned a private room right in front of the nurse's station on the ward. He won't be on monitors, but he will be on constant watch and his vitals will be checked every two hours.

Another requirement of Palo Alto is that David be able to cough on his own. We have been working with him all day, and he's doing a great job. They only had to suction him a couple of times today. This is also good news so far as brain trauma, as it shows he is instinctively clearing his passageways. I take my good news where I can find it.

I'm hoping David grows more responsive as he grows more accustomed to his pain regimen. He had been making really good progress.

It's now about 6:30... we're both pretty exhausted.

Wednesday, November 14, 2007
(Walter Reed)
It's almost 2PM, we've just come back to the Mologne House
for a late lunch.

Little David is having a really good day. This is his first day up on
the fifth floor. He has a private room near the nurse's station.
It's quiet, the staff are great.

David was a bit quiet first thing this morning, but as the
morning went on, he became much more responsive. He
blinked for the nurse when she asked him to. At one point he
moved his eyes to look at his mom. He is again focusing on
objects around the room.

During a session of physical therapy, he was looking very
attentively at the therapist as she spoke to him, focusing on
different parts of her face. She has a very kind, soothing voice.

When she was working with his left foot, she and I both saw
him move his toes. This is really great, because this is the leg
with the broken femur, and we haven't been getting much
response to pain from that foot. This was even better than
response to pain. He actually moved his toes on his own.

Palo Alto has said they will have one opening next week and
another opening the week after. I am really hoping that David's
status will be good enough that they will be willing to take him
next week. I think we may be talking with them tomorrow.

Thursday, November 15, 2007
(Walter Reed)
David had another good physical therapy session today. He was moving his toes while I was holding my hand against his left foot thru-out the session. He attempted to pull his right leg inward when the therapist asked him to. He even tried to turn his head to one side to look at the therapist.

After the session, and thru most of the rest of the day, he was pretty quiet. He did move his eyes to look at me several times, but I was unable to get him to blink on command.

Sylvia and I had a video teleconference with Palo Alto this afternoon. David will be going into their "Emerging Consciousness Program". It's a three month program. After that, further programs will depend on how David has progressed.

David will be flying Air Force Medivac from here to Travis Air Force Base, several hours drive from Palo Alto. He will be staying at a medical facility at Travis AFB overnight. The next day, he will be transported to Palo Alto. He will spend several days in their Intermediate ICU so they can monitor him to insure he handled the transfer okay. After that, he will be moved to the program.

We're waiting for the Intermediate ICU to tell us they have a bed ready for him. When they give the word, the medivac will be coordinated and we're outta here. This can happen any day.

When David makes the move to Palo Alto, he will be attached to the Wounded Warriors Brigade (or something like that) out of Fort Lewis.

Friday, November 16, 2007
(Walter Reed)
I managed to get David to blink several times for me this
morning, clearly responding to my commands. It is still
inconsistent, but it is there.

There was something really exciting today. In the morning,
David turned his head about an inch to the right to get a better
look at me.

This evening, he did the same thing, this time to get a look at
the tv. The television in this room is a small personal tv on an
articulating arm. I keep it just out of his direct line of sight,
forcing him to move his eyes to look at it. I certainly wasn't
expecting him to actually move his head. Cool.

All in all, though, David was quiet today. He looked relaxed and
comfortable.

David is all set to go to Palo Alto. The paperwork is done, and
the medivac is being lined up. We are told that it might be
Monday or Tuesday, but we should be ready in case it happens
on the weekend, but... it might be Wednesday. Sigh...

We packaged up and mailed home the boxes of gifts that David
has gotten from organizations over the past five weeks. We'll
be taking them down to Palo Alto with us so David will have
them when he wakes up.

Saturday, November 17, 2007
(Walter Reed)
We haven't heard anything more about when we're going to Palo Alto, so I'm guessing it probably won't be before Tuesday.

David is turning his head more and more often to look at things on his right side. He will also move his eyes around to study things. It looks like he's trying to process what he's seeing.

When we first went into his room this morning, I saw that the nurse had placed the tv directly in front of David. I moved it a little to the side, and David immediately turned his head toward the tv and moved his eyes (*Dad, I was watching that*).

A few minutes later, Sylvia moved to the right side of the bed and David turned his head to look at her.

David doesn't focus on anything for too long, and after turning his head, he will usually let it roll back after a few seconds, but it's the act of moving his head or his eyes to look at something that is so important.

He's also moving the toes on his left foot more and more. This is the side with the broken femur, so we're really happy to see this.

I would have liked to have seen David respond to our commands a bit more. I couldn't get him to blink on command today, and he has yet to squeeze our fingers on command. However, what we are seeing now is very encouraging. He is taking in the sights and sounds and movements around him and is processing them. You can see his mind working. He also seems to be much more responsive to me and Sylvia than to others, so I'm certain he knows who we are. I can't wait to get him to Palo Alto so the experts can begin working with him.

Sunday, November 18, 2007
(Walter Reed)
We are going to talk with family support tomorrow morning
about scheduling our own flight out of here. I'm a bit
concerned about finding seats during thanksgiving week.

Little David is still looking around the room, moving his head an
inch to one side or another when there is movement. As he has
the last few days, he isn't responding to our commands right
now. It's like he's too busy processing the world around him to
bother blinking on command. So, we'll do what we can and
leave it to the experts in Palo Alto.

He does seem to work with me when I'm doing physical
therapy with him. With continual urging, I can sometimes get
him to lower his arm a little or pull in his leg. Also, he continues
to move the foot and toes of his left leg (the one with the
broken femur).

This morning, the nurse told us that David "gave birth to two
very healthy bowel movements". Two days ago the doctors
switched David from a thinner, highly enriched food (like
Ensure) to a food with higher fiber. I guess it's working.

We'll let you know the minute we hear when David is set to fly
out.

Monday, November 19, 2007
(Walter Reed)

We're still waiting for word on the medivac. We do know that the paperwork for David's travel has progressed forward, but the medivac itself hasn't completed its manifest. We're still hoping for tomorrow.

We had been concerned that if we waited on scheduling our own flight out until we were sure David was set to go that we wouldn't be able to get seats, this being Thanksgiving week. However, Soldier Family Support told us that if we come to them in the morning, they will get us out that day, whether it's tomorrow or the next day. Okay...

Not much change in David today. Physically, he continues to get better. No fever, good heart rate, good blood pressure. We're seeing more movement in his toes and feet. He looks good.

He continues to move his head slightly to one side when there is movement or sound. He continues to focus on things around him, at least for a few seconds.

He still isn't responding to our commands, and today I again had difficulty getting him to look at me when I talked to him. But when I would move to the other side of the bed, he would turn his head slightly and look in my direction.

Tuesday, November 20, 2007
(Walter Reed)

Medivac is taking David out tomorrow morning. He'll be leaving Walter Reed at 5AM and flying out of Andrews AFB at 9AM. He will spend tomorrow night at Travis AFB in California. Palo Alto will pick him up there day after tomorrow.

David was very responsive today. He and I had several conversations, my asking fairly straightforward yes/no questions and David blinking in reply. Other times during the day he would look at me, stare directly at me with clear, sharp eyes, he looked very alert. He's definitely ready for rehab. I'm very hopeful.

Leaving him tonight was really hard, because we won't see him
now for a week. We've been at his bedside every day for more
than five weeks. This is what we've been waiting for, but that
didn't make leaving him any easier.

Sylvia and I are set to fly out at 6AM tomorrow, so we'll be at
the airport at 4AM. We've closed our orders, gotten our
itinerary, and we have our taxi voucher in hand.

The taxi ride to the airport was as strange as the trip in almost
six weeks earlier. We were up at around 2AM. We showered and
packed, went out into the lobby at 3:30 and signed out. The cab
pulled up outside the Mologne House and we gave the driver our
voucher.

This trip, the driver took the main streets to the airport, so we
saw a lot that we hadn't seen before. The streets were mostly
empty, the driver never said a word. I remember that he and the
car both smelled strongly of cigarettes.

Sylvia and I were silent for the most part. I don't think we said
much at all during that drive. Our minds were mostly on the fact
that David was no doubt being readied for his trip. He was going
to be in a medivac cargo jet an hour or so behind us as we
crossed the country. Our boy was going to be going through this
all alone. All those weeks sitting at his side, talking to him,
comforting him, and we weren't going to be there during this
scary time.

And we weren't going to be seeing him for a week.

Our plane was no doubt a bit more comfortable than David's.
It was a newer Boeing 767. Sylvia and I sat in one of the back
rows, and had the two side seats rather than the mass of seats in
the middle of the compartment.

Small television screens were set into the backs of the
headrests in front of us. At some point during the flight, Sylvia
was watching a sitcom on her screen, I had found the Discovery
Channel. The program was about a team of climbers attempting
an ascent up Mt. Everest. They were having a number of
difficulties, one of which was a less experienced team climbing
ahead of them. The weather was turning bad and time was
running out. They were trying desperately to find a way past the
slower team and make a run for the top.

But what struck me, and what would change the rest of my
life, was when the narrator mentioned that one of the climbers
had undergone back surgery a few years earlier.

The surgery had been a spinal fusion.

Just like me.

An X-Ray displayed on the screen. The fusion was in the lumbar region, the lower back.

Just like me.

And like David.

Yet this man was climbing the highest mountain on Earth.

As I sat there in the back of the plane, an idea was born fully formed in my mind. It didn't matter that my son was in a military cargo jet Medivac several hours behind us, in a vegetative state, surrounded by a medical team, his body still broken, his internal organs still struggling to heal.

It didn't matter that after six weeks he had yet to utter a word or even let us know that he was still in there.

We were flying from Washington DC to Washington State, and would be flying right past Mt. Rainier.

Which made me think... if this guy could climb the highest mountain on Earth, then my son and I could climb Mt. Rainier.

I had never climbed a mountain in my life. That didn't matter.

David had been blown up in Afghanistan a month and a half earlier, his body blasted apart in the concussive explosion, spine broken in three places with a vertebrate completely shattered. He was suffering severe traumatic brain injury and was still at the lowest level of consciousness.

None of that slowed down my thought processes one bit.

I myself was living with degenerative arthritis of the spine, had recently had a spinal fusion and knew that I was eventually going to have another. That didn't matter.

None of it mattered.

My boy was going to get better.

He and I were going to climb Mt. Rainier.

Palo Alto

Saturday, November 24, 2007
(Palo Alto)
It's early Saturday morning.

David was transported to Palo Alto yesterday.

He left Walter Reed at 5AM on Wednesday, flew out of Andrews at 9AM, arrived in Travis that afternoon.

He stayed at the ICU at Travis AFB until Friday morning, when Palo Alto came to pick him up. He's been in ICU at Palo Alto since then.

David has been running a temperature since arriving in California, and doesn't seem to be as comfortable as he was his last few days at Walter Reed. His heart rate was up for a while, but it is getting better. They're not sure if this is all from the stress of the trip or if he has developed an infection.

The plan had been for David to stay in ICU in Palo Alto until they were sure he had handled the trip okay, then move him to his program. Since he was doing so well before the trip, and not quite as well after the trip, I would guess that he could have handled it better.

They will move him from ICU as soon as they've resolved these issues.

As of now, Sylvia and I are still planning to drive down in a few days.

Thursday, November 29, 2007
(Palo Alto)
Last email before we drive down to Palo Alto (leaving at 4AM).

I talked with the ICU attending doc for about an hour this afternoon. We hadn't talked before and he called to fill me in on all that has been happening with David. I had heard much of this before with the other docs and nurses, but it was good to get a complete rundown from head to foot from the ICU doc in charge.

They do plan on removing the external pins and bracing on David's femur next week, but they want to keep the neck brace on him for a while longer (was supposed to come off a couple of days ago).

David hasn't had a fever for a few days, and the infections are diminishing. The doc says that he could have left ICU three days ago, but they wanted to keep an eye on his vitals as he fought the infections and made the switch from morphine to methadone. (We got word this PM that David will be moving to Intermediate ICU tomorrow and general ward in a couple of days. After a few days there, he will go into the program).

One thing the doctor is concerned about is the continual clinching of his hands. This wasn't much of a problem at Walter Reed because I worked with him every day while we were there and the occupational physical therapist came in daily. The doctor says he's upset that physical therapy hasn't been coming into ICU to work with David regularly.

Sem and the kids got to Palo Alto today. They told us that when they went in to see David, he turned his head and opened his

eyes wide. When they told us, Sylvia started crying. David
hasn't been as responsive at Palo Alto as he was when we were
with him at Walter Reed. It's great that he has family with him
again. I can't wait to see him tomorrow.

David would spend seven months at Palo Alto, which is about
a thousand miles from our little town outside Olympia,
Washington; about 16 hours by car, depending on traffic and
weather. Sylvia and I would make ten trips over those seven
months. We usually took two days driving down, mostly a timing
issue. No matter what time we left home, if I drove straight
through we usually ended up in really bad commuter traffic when
we got anywhere near Palo Alto (meaning Oakland, San
Francisco, San Jose). So after the first few trips, we began
stopping about 10-12 hours down and then finishing the drive to
Palo Alto the next morning, getting in around 10AM (in between
the morning and lunch traffic crunches). Coming home, we
usually made the drive in one day, despite the fact that Sylvia
doesn't drive. I just made sure to take a break every couple of
hours. There are a lot of really nice rest stops along I-5.

The army paid for our gas, so that helped some. And they
allotted some money for hotels while we were there, though this
wasn't nearly enough. Living in Palo Alto is very expensive. Even
some of the doctors and nurses who worked with David lived
outside the area, saying that only computer people could afford to
live in town.

Anyway, we tried a hotel once for the rate the army paid us,
and decided never again. So we often ended up paying $150 or so
per night out of our own pocket, above the army per diem;
sometimes more, if there was something going on in the area.

Sem made it to Palo Alto a few days before we did. She and the
kids spent a brief time in a hotel before getting into the Fisher
House.

The Fisher House was great. Right across the lawn from the
polytrauma unit, it's a place for families to stay while dealing with
having a loved one at the hospital or polytrauma. We got to know
a number of families staying there, and there were several that
Sylvia and I knew from our time at Walter Reed.

Having the Fisher House available meant that Sem was able to
just walk across the street each day to be with David. And you
could see the Fisher House from his window.

Each of our ten trips down lasted about a week. With two and
a half days travel time, that gave us four days or so with David.

This was a lot less than we wanted, but we just couldn't afford more. We're not wealthy, and even with the partial support we got from the army, by the time David left Palo Alto we would end up about $10,000 in debt, and we're still struggling to get out of that hole.

So far as time away from work, my office was very understanding. I used up all my sick leave and annual leave during our time at Walter Reed, but a lot of people donated "shared leave", giving up some of their own leave time for me, which gave me the time for the Palo Alto trips. For Sylvia, though, it was all time lost, and this made our growing debt even worse.

Of course, none of that mattered to us. I don't remember Sylvia and me ever even discussing it at the time. It wasn't until David was back up here in Washington State that we took enough of a breather to sit down and talk about how we might pay all this back. What it came down to mostly was that we would tighten our belts, wouldn't be making some big ticket purchases that we had planned on, and we wouldn't be retiring anytime soon.

So, a week or so in Palo Alto, a week or two at home, then do it all again. For seven months.

Several of our drives down were exciting in and of themselves. In order to get from here to there, you have to drive over the Siskiyous, and beyond that through Shasta. During the winter, both of these stretches of I-5 can be treacherous, and on several occasions they were. A couple of times we had to stop when the pass closed ahead of us. Once on the way home we found ourselves all alone. It turned out that we were the last car they let through before closing the pass on both ends. That was a really rough drive.

All in all, about half our trips were made through snow and ice, at least to some degree. If it hadn't been that we were going to see Little David, there's no way we would have even attempted it.

We did try flying down once. It was our second trip. We didn't know any better. It turned out to be a big mistake, for a number of reasons.

The drive up to SeaTac Airport from our house is about an hour and a half. Parking is upwards to $35 a day, or you can drive up the night before, spend a couple of hundred for a hotel and then store your car in the hotel's parking lot for $15 a day. Airport security was difficult to say the least, and so we spent another couple of hours at SeaTac before flying out. We arrived in San Jose, found our way to the shuttles, and then had to wait for a bus to take us to the rent-a-car lots. There was another line, check-in, get the car, and get on our way; only to find that traffic from the San Jose airport to Palo Alto is awful, no matter what time of day you're traveling.

If we had made the trip down by car rather than air, we'd have been half way there and wouldn't have had any of the nightmare.

After all that, we discovered that the army wasn't going to recoup us for airfare, parking and rentals. They would cover gas expenses, so long as we supplied receipts, and hotel stays for up to a certain amount.

That was the one and only time we took the plane.

When we arrived in Palo Alto on that first trip, David was in the main building of the Veteran's Hospital, up in Intermediate ICU (IICU). From his window, you could see the single-story polytrauma unit building down below, and the Fisher House beyond that.

Several of the staff in the IICU were conscientious and caring. Many, however, saw no reason to go out of their way in keeping David clean and comfortable. To them he was little more than a vegetable, and what was the point in cleaning his mess or brushing his teeth?

We also found that no one from therapy at polytrauma was coming up to see him. It turned out that they didn't like having to deal with the IICU staff.

I got hold of the ICU doctor that I had been in long-distance communication with. He came down to IICU and we talked. He wasn't any happier than we were, and I do think this was genuine. He made a bit of a scene, and promised that David was going to be properly looked after. He was also going to talk with the head of the polytrauma unit and see that David received therapy during his time in IICU.

Sylvia and I felt very uncomfortable about leaving Palo Alto a few days later with David still not in polytrauma.

Wednesday, December 12, 2007
(Palo Alto)
Well, when Sem went in to see David yesterday morning, she was ecstatic to see him out of the neck brace and no feeding tube in his nose. Then she found out that he had vomited during the night. Some of us are thinking that he may have had a reaction to one of the medications. The two antibiotics he's on now are different than what he's been taking in the past.

Sem took the opportunity to shave him, and she says he looks so good. Clean shaven and without the neck brace and the tubes, he looks normal again.

He didn't have a fever in the morning, but when we talked with Sem again last night she said that it had crept back up to a little over a hundred.

One doctor was talking to Sem about finally putting the peg back in his abdomen. Later, she couldn't get a definitive answer from the attending physician. I think this would be great; keep that feeding tube out of nose. I'm guessing the only reason they are finally getting about putting it back in is because they can't have the feeding tube in his nose and down his throat if they think he might vomit. For the moment, they are feeding him via IV, which is not a good long-term solution for a number of reasons.

So now I have no idea when David is going down to rehab, and I'm not comfortable with him being in Palo Alto's Intermediate ICU. I don't think it's up to same standard as Walter Reed. The brain trauma unit, however, if he ever gets there, is probably the best facility in the country. That's where he needs to be.

Sem says that she's doing okay. The kids started school down there on Monday. That has to be good for them and it makes life easier for Sem.

Friday, December 14, 2007
(Palo Alto)
The doctors did a biopsy on his leg. There is no sign of infection, but there is an indication of additional bone growth. They don't have much experience with this, and are bringing in an expert to have a look. Not sure what's going on with this one...

They did an MRI on his brain. From what I understand, the only abnormality they found is that there is still some minor swelling. They think it is possible that this is the source of the ongoing fever.

The neurologists have asked for a spinal fluid draw, and this is happening this afternoon. It may give some further clues into the brain trauma and what may still be going on there, including the fever.

They told Sem that unless the results of the spinal fluid draw indicate otherwise, David will be moved to rehab early next week, perhaps as early as Monday. I'm glad I decided not to hold my breath the last six times they told us that.

I think that come Monday, we'll know a lot more about the path Little David is going to be taking.

We did have one really, really good sign yesterday. David yawned when the physical therapist team from the brain trauma unit was there. They took one look inside his mouth and went to the nursing staff demanding to know why they haven't been cleaning his mouth and teeth. Later, after they left, the nurse came in, looked at David's closed mouth and made some offhand comment about not knowing how she was going to be able to do this... Sem leaned over David and told him to open his mouth. She told him again. The third time she told him to open his mouth, he did. That's absolutely amazing. Sem told the nurse she could clean his mouth now. Apparently, from David's facial expressions, he wasn't too happy about having his mouth cleaned.

Thursday, December 20, 2007
(Palo Alto)
Well, I finally got them to move Little David over to the rehab
unit.

They haven't been able to start him on his program yet,
because he's still having half a dozen different medical issues.
At least he's in an environment that focuses on his mental
recovery, and I think he's on track to clear up the medical stuff.

I talked with some of the staff down there yesterday, trying to
sort out the schedule and some of the specific things they're
going to be doing with him. I don't have all the answers yet, as I
wasn't able to talk with the doctor assigned to oversee his
recovery (I did see him when I was down there earlier). I'm
scheduled to talk with him this afternoon.

I'm really hoping for some exciting news over the next few
days. However long his recovery might be, the first step will be
an amazing one.

The atmosphere around the Fisher House and the polytrauma
unit at Christmas time was really quiet. The dining room in the
Fisher House had a large tree in the corner. There was another in
the main room. The kids got presents. People tried, but the whole
scene seemed very surreal to me.

David's birthday is December 27th, and as he was growing up
Sylvia and I worked hard to make sure that he had both a
Christmas and a birthday. And we strongly encouraged people
not to give him a single "combined Christmas and birthday"
present.

This year was tough. We focused a lot on the kids, our
daughter's two girls back in Washington State and David's kids
living there at the Fisher House, but we also tried to give David
his Christmas and his birthday. He seemed increasingly aware of
his surroundings during this time, but as I look back, I don't
really know how much he understood of what specifically was
going on. Did he really make the connection between the
celebration and Christmas, singing happy birthday on his
birthday? I don't know whether we'll ever know for sure.

Saturday, December 29, 2007
(Palo Alto)
David's schedule involves "Rest Periods" before and after his
therapy sessions.

Before his speech therapy, he needs to have half an hour of
quiet time so that when the pathologist comes in she can get
his full attention. He can't be excited or trying to deal with
other issues.

He has half an hour between speech therapy and physical
therapy. This time has also been designated as Rest Period. This
is because it is vitally important that David's brain have time to
sort out and organize the information from the speech session.

The therapists want David to have at least an hour Rest Period
after the physical therapy session, for two reasons. The first is
that David tires very easily and needs to rest, and second, he
again needs to have time for his brain to sort thru the
experience.

Physical therapy has been adding a second session in the
afternoon, this primarily involving getting him into his
wheelchair and out of his room. The target for now is one hour
in the chair in the afternoon. I believe they will be adding more
activities to this second session as David can tolerate it.

Yesterday, the speech therapist told me she wanted to start
two sessions a day. We tried an afternoon session, but he had
already had a busy day and we kept it to only about twenty
minutes.

I asked to be kept as involved in David's different sessions as
could be allowed, and they have included me in all his sessions.
They know how involved I was with David at Walter Reed and
maybe sense how outside of it I've been feeling here.

Yesterday, they put David on the tilt table for the first time.
This is where they strap him to the table and tilt the table up.
This is an important step in getting him to stand up. They
checked his blood pressure at different degrees along the way,
prepared to stop if the pressure rose or fell more than they

were comfortable with. Remember, he's been lying down since
October 12 and his system isn't used to blood going to the feet.

To help keep him calm, I stood in front of him, held his hand
and talked with him. His blood pressure did very well until he
was at about 70%, which was the target for the day. They
lowered him back to the previous step, and his blood pressure
was better than mine. He did very, very well. They told me he
did better than they could have hoped for.

During the morning speech therapy session, the therapist had
Sylvia and I stand apart at the foot of the bed and asked David
to look at his Mom. You could see him attempting to move his
eyes and head from me to Sylvia. The therapist also held
pictures in front of him and was asking him if the picture was of
one person or another, looking for David to indicate yes or no
in whatever way he seemed to be comfortable with. She is still
trying to come up with the best way for him to communicate
with us. She focused again on eyebrow raises and head raises,
the two actions he seems to be most comfortable with. She felt
pretty good about David's eyebrow raises, but it still isn't
consistent.

David laughed during the session. Sylvia showed him the
picture of him putting his face into his birthday cake from a
couple of years ago. She reminded him how he had Kevin and
Ashley dig into the cake, and then afterward, as they were
cleaning up, his dog Trixie decided it was her turn.

Also during this session, as I was standing on his right side and
talking with him, David tried to look over at me and lift himself
up. He has trouble looking over to this side.

The abbreviated afternoon session didn't do much for
communication, but some of other responses were uplifting for
us.

We are seeing him work his mouth more and more, swallow
more and more. The speech therapist has brought this up a
couple of times.

Following the afternoon session, Sylvia and I went to the
speech therapist's office and met with her for about an hour.

This is where we got a lot of information about the progress she feels she has seen with him over the last four weeks and where she sees the program going from her perspective. She has seen a lot of progress and is hopeful.

While we were in our meeting, the physical therapists put David into his chair and brought him out into the Day Room to spend some time with his Grandma and Grandpa. This was great, because they're only here for a few days and like I said, our time with him is more limited now that he's in the program.

The doctors have indicated that they are going to begin training David away from the trach. Sometime in the next week they will start blocking the tube for a few minutes at a time to encourage him to breathe through his nose. After a week or two they will remove the trach.

One of the doctors also indicated during one meeting that they are looking ahead to feeding him through his mouth. This of course will require the trach to be removed.

It's 6AM Saturday and I need to get ready to go to the trauma unit.

Monday, December 31, 2007
(Palo Alto)
David had a busy weekend.

He had quite a few visitors come by to see him, and we continued to see positive responses. During each visit, even if he began quiet, he usually perked up. He took the visits well and never appeared agitated. Rather, he seemed to enjoy them. He continues to laugh occasionally at a comment or a situation.

Some time ago, we were told that with brain trauma patients, you just never know what is going to trigger a response, or indeed a full return. We saw further indications of this on Saturday. One was where my brother and sister came to see David. He hadn't seen them since he was a young teenager. Tom was telling David about the time David's cousin Joey wore a devil's Halloween costume, red horns and all. David broke out into the largest, most emotional laugh I've seen. His face was bright and cheery, his mouth was a huge grin from ear to ear. If David hadn't had the trach, it would have been one of those rip-roaring laughs. A minute later, Tom reminded David how his sister Christy had responded to Joey's costume. Tom used hand and face gestures. David was watching him and he laughed again, just as expressively. He was smiling throughout most of Tom and Terri's visit.

Something else I saw David do with Tom. Tom asked David a question and I saw David nod his head. It was little more than a twitch, but it was clearly an affirmative nod. I was very surprised, but didn't say anything at first. I told myself that I needed to see this again for "verification". Tom on the other hand, not knowing that this was something David had never done before, took it for granted and so he asked David another question. David nodded a second time. Again, it was brief, but very much a nod.

This all reminded me that when David and Christy were young, the families often got together on Sundays. These were usually very loud family affairs, football on the television, the kids running around under foot. I know that some of my own most pleasant childhood memories were those of family get-togethers where the grownups spent the day sitting around the table arguing loudly and the cousins ran about playing, for the most part ignoring the grownups. David may have similar memories about our own family get-togethers, and Tom's reappearance after all these years may have brought them back.

I know I have a picture of Joey with that devil's costume around somewhere. I will look for it.

Something else that clearly shows that David listens to what is going on around him and understands and processes what he hears. This comes in two parts. The first occurred when his therapists were transferring him from his bed to his chair. The woman's scrub pants began to slide off her hips and she commented that she was losing her pants. David laughed so hard he began coughing and phlegm shot out of his trach and across the room. That initial reaction is great, but there is more. Later, after the physical therapy session was over and

David had been returned to his bed, I was standing beside the bed telling Leonard about what had happened earlier. I had gotten into the story to the point where I was just about to tell of the therapist's scrubs starting to slip down, and David starting laughing again. He knew what I was about to say.

David is also spending more time in the gym. Physical therapy loads him up in his chair and takes him into the gym, where he is placed on a raised mat table. They go through all the familiar exercises, but now also include exercises with him sitting up on the edge of the table. Sem is working closely with the therapists during these sessions.

David doesn't have speech therapy sessions on the weekends, but I'm hoping that with his continuing progress over the last few days, he'll show just as much communication progress when these resume today.

Thursday, January 10, 2008
(Palo Alto)
I haven't written anything for a few days, mostly because things have been rather quiet.

He still does not actively communicate, and the speech therapist has still not established the best way to get this going.

David does continue to be aware of the world around him and he often responds. He will react to people talking to him, usually by moving his eyes and looking at them. When Sem says that Mom or Dad is on the phone, he will lift his eyebrows. He did seem to respond to his Mom telling him stories over the phone of when he and his sister were young.

Sem says that when she watches TV with him in the evening, he focuses on the program.

The doctors are trying to wean him away from the trach in his throat, encouraging him to breathe through his nose. It may still be another week or more before they can remove the trach.

Sem takes him outside most days in his wheelchair. She says she thinks he likes this. He of course is still not standing on his own, or even sitting up. They are simulating these things in his physical therapy, but for now it's his bed or the wheelchair.

We'll be back down with him next week. I'm taking his sister down with us. They were very close growing up, and he seems to respond very well to memories of when he was young. I'm not putting any pressure on Christy, but who knows... this may take him to that next step. He's been right there for several weeks, standing at the line but just not crossing over. They tell us again and again that you never know what is going to trigger responses or how far he might go.

Saturday, January 19, 2008
(Palo Alto)
Saturday 6AM:

We came in yesterday (Friday) morning and went right to David's room.

He's been moved to a larger room with a window that looks out onto the grounds and he can see the Fisher House where Sem and the kids are staying.

David looks good. His arms are less constricted than a few weeks ago, and physically he just looks healthier.

He seems very alert and very curious about everything going on around him. However, I found it difficult to get him to focus on anything for more than a second or two.

Sem told me something and I saw it happen yesterday during his occupational therapy.

We all know how stubborn David can be. Well, when the occupational therapists are working him, he will just lay there as if totally unaware. Once they leave, he perks right up. Sem told me about this, and says that he will smirk once they're out of the room. Yesterday, I saw them getting almost nothing out of David, and after they left, Sem looked down at him and said "you did that on purpose". I saw him smile at her and laugh.

We talked for some time with the speech therapist, and she said that she has called him on this. She said that since then she and David have begun building a relationship and are now making really good progress. She said that she is getting to know him and this is helping a lot.

Now for some really good news...

The speech therapist's sessions have been including getting David's vocal chords working. She puts a device on his trach that allows him to breathe in through the trach but forces him to breathe out through his nose and mouth. I watched a session yesterday and she does have a good relationship with him.

When working on this, she will try to get him to use his voice. His vocal chords are open right now and she is trying to bring them closed.

During the morning session, she told David that if he wanted her to stop that he needed to tell her to stop.

She said that he clearly said "stop".

I was with her and David during yesterday's afternoon session. Midway through she asked me to speak with him. I knelt in front of him and said "Hi, David".

David made a serious attempt at saying "hi". It was more of a heavy breathing out, but was clearly an attempt to make a sound in response to me.

The speech therapist told us that David can be very responsive to her, particularly nodding yes. Shaking his head no is less certain.

Christy spent some time with David talking about some of their adventures growing up. He was very responsive to this and there was a lot of laughing. Sylvia got a lot of similar responses. His sense of humor is there.

We did have a problem last night. David is now fed through the stomach peg on a set feeding schedule rather than a constant feed. During his evening "meal" it became plugged. Specialists spent the evening trying to identify what was wrong. As of late in the evening, it hadn't been resolved. He was going in for scans.

We should find out this morning about what they are going to do. He may have to have the feeding tube inserted through his nose short term. I hope not. This could impact his speech therapy.

I should have something more this evening or tomorrow morning.

Sunday, January 20, 2008
(Palo Alto)
Sunday 8PM:

It's Sunday evening (about 8PM) and Sylvia and I have just returned to our room.

Yesterday morning when we got to the hospital, the night nurse stopped us to tell us that she managed to clear David's stomach peg overnight, David got fed and received meds around midnight.

I got to be with David when he went on the tilt table. They had him nearly standing up for 25 minutes. He was occasionally anxious (frightened), but we looked into each other's eyes throughout the session and his heart rate and blood pressure showed that he took it pretty well.

He was quite emotional much of the day. At times it was almost heartbreaking, and in the evening, once David quieted down, Sylvia and I spent several quiet hours with him before returning to our hotel late in the evening.

We spent the entire day with David again today. He was a bit anxious again this morning, but calmed down about 10AM. We sat quietly with him until around 1PM, when he was lifted into his wheelchair and taken to the gym. We went with him, and the therapist had us assist, helping to keep him calm. He sat up on the edge of the padded platform for almost half an hour as they worked with him. I knelt in front of him and talked with him. The therapist asked David to look at his mom as he tried to straighten his neck. He did glance over once.

I held up two cards, one with "K" and one with "B", and the therapist asked David to look at the "K". He did, twice in a row. A minute later though, David refused to look at either one.

David and I watched the football playoffs this afternoon. He was fairly quiet and only occasionally looked at the television.

He was calm when we left him a few minutes ago. His nurse this evening is very good with him and David seems to listen to him. I think he'll have a good night.

Wednesday, January 23, 2008
(Palo Alto)
Just a quick note.

As you know, the therapist is putting the device on David's trach that allows him to breathe in thru the trach while forcing him to breathe out thru his nose and mouth. It is during this time that she encourages him to speak, attempting to retrain his vocal chords and draw them closed.

I guess that today Sem stood off to one side, out of David's line of sight as he sat in his wheelchair with the device on his trach. She kept repeating "David. David. David." I guess he got a bit irritated and said "What?"

Kinda cool.

Friday, January 25, 2008
(Palo Alto)
We just got some good news and we're going a bit crazy right
now.

A few minutes ago David's therapists put some crushed ice into
his mouth and he sucked on the ice. They gave him some more
and he chewed on the ice and swallowed. Then they gave him
some water and he drank it. They told Sem that this was a huge
step forward. They're going to try it again this afternoon at
3:00.

This is great. I can't stop Sylvia from crying. Okay, maybe I'm
doing a little crying, too.

Tuesday, January 29, 2008
(Palo Alto)
We heard a couple of things from Sem yesterday.

First of all, they are continuing to give David juice and water,
and he continues to drink. They are talking about giving him
pudding by the end of the week.

Second, they swapped out his trach with another that doesn't
have a "balloon" and allows him to breathe through his nose
and mouth all the time, without them having to deflate
anything.

This has created a bit of a situation. With this new trach, David
can now make sounds.

We're not talking interactive communication, but...

If you'll remember, David often gets upset with the therapists.
He can now do more than give them dirty looks. Sem says he
makes sounds at them, and she thinks he's cussing at them.

She says she's embarrassed. I am not. I hope he cusses up a
freakin' storm.

Monday, February 04, 2008
(Palo Alto)
Sylvia and I made it in to Palo Alto Sunday late afternoon, but
not without some difficulty.

We left home midday Saturday, once Sylvia got off work early.
We started seeing snow right away, particularly at the Black
Hills and then more so south of Olympia. Portland wasn't bad
when we went through but we heard they got a lot of snow
later.

We had to stop for the night in Medford, Oregon when they
closed the Siskiyous. The next morning we took on the pass.
Chains were required unless you had four wheel drive and
snow tires. That's us. We took it slow and made it without
much problem. It was a long drive, lots of snow, lots of
compact ice, a lot of really big trucks going really, really slow.

We had to do it all again through Shasta, and it wasn't clear
until we got about twenty miles from Redding.

It was all worth with it once we saw David.

Sem had him in his chair waiting for us outside the unit. He saw
us walking along the sidewalk and up the walkway to him. He
looked sharp and alert.

Back in the room, I noticed several things right off. He's holding
his head up much straighter, so it's not pulled down to the side.
His arms and hands aren't nearly as constricted. Also, his eyes
are so clear and sharp and he will look right at you.

We spent three hours or so with him last night before coming
here to the hotel. During that time he appeared responsive to
much of what was going on around him. I really think he knows
and understands a lot of what he sees and hears.

I asked him some pointed yes / no questions and asked him to
tell me yes or no. I really thought he was going to a couple of
times.

I said "Hi, David" and asked him to say "Hi, Dad". It looked like
he was going to.

We also noticed him moving his right arm about, placing his fingers up to his face several times. Really cool, though, was when he used his arm and hand to catch our attention or indicate that he didn't want us to leave.

It's Monday morning now and Sylvia and I are heading back over. We'll be talking with the speech therapist and physical therapists, but mostly we just want to spend time with David.

I'll send out another email tonight or tomorrow morning.

Tuesday, February 05, 2008
(Palo Alto)
It's early Tuesday morning, Sylvia and I are getting ready to go over and spend the day with David.

Yesterday was a busy day, but normal for David. He had two sessions with the speech therapist and one with the occupational therapists.

In the morning session with speech, David worked on chewing (ice) and swallowing (water, apple juice, apple sauce). His therapist also worked with David on breathing.

The afternoon session involved a lot of the same, but they also had him hold the cup of ice and juice (mostly with their help) and had him using the straw.

In both sessions David did very well with his swallowing and seemed to respond to his therapist's requests. In the afternoon session, she started David on tongue exercises using a lollipop, and after a slow start I think he got better.

The occupational therapy session had David going into the gym. The therapists had David help them get him out of his chair by having him "stand" as they lifted him up and onto the mat platform. He got a bit anxious but the therapist said she could feel his legs shaking as he tried to help.

David did well during this session as well. He was sitting on the edge of the platform and leaning forward. They asked him to lift himself up and straighten. He did this twice in a row.

Also, an important milestone happened during this session. As they were finishing up, his therapist told him he did a great job and gave him the thumbs up sign. In response, David gave the thumbs up. Big, big step.

A couple of other things yesterday...

They have been "capping" his trach for longer periods every day.

During this time, David has no choice but to breathe through his nose and mouth. The last few days have been nine hour stretches. Yesterday was going to be longer (he still had it capped when we left last night). They're going for twenty four hours today or tomorrow. If he does well, they're going to take out the trach.

Also yesterday, Sem, Kevin, Sylvia and I were hitting a balloon back and forth in David's room, occasionally hitting it to David. With just a little encouragement, David made attempts at lifting his arm and hitting it back.

Finally, David has been lifting his right hand up to his face. After doing this several times during his occupational therapy session, actually touching his eye, the therapist noticed that he had an eyelash in his eye. She said that this was as much autonomic as intentional, but is very important on her "rating scale" in which she measures David's consciousness level.

Thursday, February 07, 2008
(Palo Alto)
Just a couple of updates...

David's trach has been kept capped for several days now, and they may be removing the trach today. I should hear something soon on this. If they don't do it today, it won't happen until next week. They don't like doing things like this on a Friday.

Next... since giving his occupational therapist the "thumbs up" sign the other day, David has given me the thumbs up several times. The action in itself is very good. If he can do this consistently, we will have something really, really important. This could be a true method of communication.

David continues to do well during his speech therapy sessions as far as swallowing. How well he does here is one of the key factors in removing his trach (along with his ability to cough and the condition of his lungs). David has now had ice, water, juice, pudding, apple sauce, jello and ice cream. His eating and drinking is still confined to his speech therapy sessions as part of his swallowing and tongue exercises.

David continues to lift his right arm, seemingly to perform actions and to call attention to something. As I said before, the other day it appeared he was bothered by eyelashes and was attempting to get rid of what was bothering him.

Recently, I think he tried to let us know that he was thirsty.

After a morning session in which he was given water, juice and jello, we took him outside to sit in the sun and take in the view. After some time had passed, during which he was very alert to things going on around him, and in which he gave me a thumbs up in response to a question, David lifted his hand up to his mouth. He was moving his lips and he nodded when we asked him if he was thirsty. Since at this point only the speech therapist can put anything into his mouth, we took him back in and went looking for her. Couldn't find her, had to settle for a snuck in ice chip and the nurse gave him water thru his stomach peg.

Finally, I have confirmed from a number of the therapists that when David gets upset with them he will quite clearly mouth cuss words at them. He is an E7 (Sergeant First Class) in the army after all.

I keep saying this, but I think David is really close to clearly and consistently communicating with us. On this trip, every time that Sylvia or I sat and talked with him, he looked as though he was about to talk to us, that he was struggling to sort out what he had to do to speak. With his trach capped and soon to be removed, and with the swallowing and tongue exercises that he has been getting from the speech therapist, I think that it will happen very soon. When it does, if I am not already there I will be at his bedside 12 ½ hours after I hear about it.

Tuesday, February 12, 2008
(Palo Alto)
David had his trach removed on Thursday, and his breathing has been fine.

Up to now, we've been able to take David out onto a small patio for an hour when the weather is good. Sem now has permission to take David for walks, so she's been wheeling him around the grounds. She says that she thinks he's enjoying the change.

Sem has also been given permission to give David ice chips and water three times a day. The speech therapist "trained" her and gave her the go-ahead (The primary purpose for giving him liquids is to train him to swallow, which is why it is part of the speech therapy).

I guess Sylvia and I are to be "trained" next week when we go back down.

We've talked with David's comrades-in-arms over the past few months, and gotten to know some of them pretty well. Over the last few days, though, we've finally begun hearing a bit more about David's life in Afghanistan from their perspective (rather than what he used to tell me), as well as more about the day of the IED blast:

They felt totally alone over there. They were a very small training unit assigned to train Afghani police in the small villages; seven soldiers (officers and high-ranking sergeants, mostly), with almost no protection. All the Marines are in Iraq.

They were sometimes so isolated that the only real food they had was from the care packages that Sylvia sent them. We knew that David always shared what we sent over, so we had begun increasing the quantity...

A quote: "We were sent over there to train people. We found ourselves killing people."

Some of the guys said that David and the major (I'm withholding his name) were like "husband and wife", always bickering back and forth. The major knew what buttons to push to get David going. I know they had a strong comradeship from all the conversations we've had with the major since this happened. This has hit them all really hard. We sometimes find ourselves comforting them.

When they were hit with the IED blast and began taking on fire, David told the others to leave him behind. This is particularly telling, since I know that David's greatest fear was to be taken prisoner.

Once they finally got David out on medivac, it took several days to get the rest of the team out. Rescue teams going in to retrieve them continually took on fire.

That's just some of what we've picked up the last few days. I thought you'd like to hear it.

I'm asked now and then about pictures. I'm inserting a couple below, the boy that I remember and the man the rest of the world sees (the major is in the last picture). I hope they forward to you okay. Let me know if they don't.

By the way, David's wedding anniversary was yesterday. Sem was really down. Sylvia told her to give David a hug and appreciate that at least you're with him.

Tuesday, February 19, 2008
(Palo Alto)
Physical therapy came into David's room on Sunday.

David was apparently having one of his "no" days. He does that once in a while. He wanted nothing to do with the therapists or their plans for him. He wasn't using the word "no", but continually shook his head no and refused to do anything they asked or to help in any way. They finally backed out and left.

Sem began giving David a stern talking-to. She told him that he has to let them work with him if he wants to get better and go home.

Now... we were warned ahead of time that what David did next is very common for brain trauma patients...

David said, quite loudly and clearly... "F-U" (you fill in the missing letters).

This is quite out of character for David (at least when he's not in the hills of Afghanistan). He doesn't talk like that around his family, and he certainly doesn't speak that way to Sem (actually, no one does...). But like I said, using emotionally charged language is common for recovering brain trauma patients.

And... he spoke! And it was a two-word sentence!

It may not have been appropriate language, and not something most spouses say to each other, but it certainly articulated his thoughts at the moment.

Also, it wasn't nonsensical. It wasn't like someone asking David how he was and he responding with "dinosaurs". It may have been poor taste, bad manners, and out of character, but it made some sense...

Sem quickly recovered from the shock and said "Your Mom and Dad are coming. Are you going to talk like that in front of your Mom?"

David thought a moment, looked Sem in the eye and said, loud and clear, "No".

And that was it. He was done for the day.

When Sem talked to us a little bit later, having had time to think about it, she was getting excited about it. David had been whispering a word or two every now and then for a few days, but nothing that she could understand. This... this they understood all the way down the hall. It was that loud and that distinct.

She says he's calmer now, and quieter.

Sylvia and I are heading out tomorrow for our next trip down. I want so much to walk into his room and hear him say "Hi, Dad." I'll take anything, but the day I hear that will be the best day of my life. It will be the bookend to October 12, 2007... the worst day.

I'll send an email from Palo Alto.

Tuesday, February 26, 2008
(Palo Alto)
I got to spend quite a bit of time alone with Little David on this last trip down. He and I would spend quiet time, or talk (I would, anyway), or even watch some TV (When watching television, there are times I believe he understands at least some of what he is watching. I know that he enjoys it).

Sem told Sylvia that "when David is with his Dad, he goes into Little Boy mode".

Well, I think I go into Daddy mode. David looks at me so "completely". His look and expression show such contentment and trust, and his gaze goes so deep, that it draws me in. And he will purse his lips together the way he did when he was young and give this deep, contented sigh. It's my little boy laying there. I want to reach over and pull him to me and take him back in time to before all this happened.

His speech therapist says that he is so clearly and obviously a family oriented person, and that his mood and responses are completely different when he has his family around him

Each trip down, one of the physical therapists tells me that he wants me there for all the PT sessions because he can get so much more from David when his dad is there.

During the last PT session before we left Palo Alto, they put David into a "standing frame" in which they strap David in and lift him to his feet, set his arms onto a shelf. The standing frame is "graduating up" from the tilt table they were putting David onto before. We had the whole family in there and I think it helped David quite a bit. He "stood" for 25 minutes.

Also, I asked if it would be all right if we ate lunch as a family when they bring David's pureed lunch in. The therapist thought it was a great idea, so for the last two days of our trip David sat at a table with Sem, Sylvia and me for lunch. Sem doesn't actually get to eat much, because she's feeding David. We're not seeing too much yet so far as interaction, but he seems at ease and he's eating well.

Sem told me last night that they are going to begin the water therapy sessions today. She went out and bought him some new swimming trunks for the occasion. I imagine that he will be a bit anxious the first time, just as he has been for each new therapy. I'm waiting for Sem's call to find out how it went.

We'll be going back down this weekend and hope to spend a few more days there than the last few trips. I've blocked out two 10 day periods for March, though I don't know how many days I will actually be able to be down there. A lot of it depends on Sylvia's schedule.

Monday, March 05, 2008
(Palo Alto)
I should have been in Palo Alto as of yesterday, but because of
some medical problems, I wasn't able to travel down. I'm
supposed to stay at home for a few days. We'll see what
happens.

Talking with David's primary doctor (head of the medical staff
at the trauma unit), he says he's very happy with what he sees.
I'd like to see more, but hey, the doc's happy...

We've been a bit concerned about David appearing overly tired
the last few days, but the doctor says he thinks that David's
brain is working through the night and he's not sleeping much.
They think that when the nursing staff comes in to check on
him, that David is closing his eyes in an attempt to ignore them,
and that's why they are logging him in as "sleeping".

Sem is feeding David his meals more and more (pureed, of
course). So long as David continues to eat well, he doesn't get
fed through the tube. He is down another pound though, and
they are going to put him on a "high calorie diet".

Sem got permission to take David over to the Fisher House
where she and the kids are staying (right across the street from
the trauma unit), for "visits". She wants to have him over there
in the evenings to sit with the kids when they're doing
homework or whatever, while she cooks dinner, and then to sit
with them for family dinners.

The other day when the nursing staff were using the lift to
swing David from his bed to the chair, they had some trouble
getting David swung around and they smacked his leg against
the lift. This wasn't the first time. Not all the staff there are
skilled at using the lift. David got upset and said to one of the
nurses "you're stupid".

This indicates that David is getting better about translating his
thoughts into words. But... it also indicates that the part of his
brain that controls restraining speaking whatever you're
thinking isn't yet working.

One more item... today Sem told us that when she saw that
David had a runny nose, she handed him a tissue. He took the
tissue and wiped at his nose.

Wednesday, March 12, 2008
(Palo Alto)
A couple of things going on with David, some happening over
the last few days, some I just heard a couple of minutes ago.

David has been on pureed food for a little while now, and has
been doing well enough that they haven't had to give him
Ensure through his stomach peg. Today they gave him his first
solid food. He did so well with this that they are now talking
about moving him completely off the pureed food and are
saying that they may soon remove the stomach peg.

Sem says that this weekend we will all be sitting in the dining
room at the Fisher House with David, all having the same food.

The other day Sem went to the store and bought David a pair
of shoes (optimism!). When she got back to David's room, she
held up the shoes and said "Look, David... I bought you new
shoes." David was sitting in his wheelchair. He lifted his foot for
her to put on his new shoes. For him to do that, there had to be
a lot of brain processing going on.

One sad item that may become good news...

Medical staff periodically explain to David where he is, why he
is there, and how he came by his injuries. When they ask David
if he remembers what happened to him in Afghanistan, he
emphatically shakes his head no. I've seen him sternly deny
what they are saying as they tell him of the IED blast and what
happened afterward.

Today, Sem sat with him and told him what had happened. As
with the medical staff, he shook his head no. He didn't
remember it. It didn't happen. She firmly explained that it did
happen, and she detailed what happened and how he came to
be where he is.

It took some time, but then David began to cry. Then of course, Sem began to cry. I guess she held onto him for a long time.

Maybe this will help. At the very least, David may now actually understand where he is and why he is there. And, just maybe, this may accelerate his cognitive healing.

Sunday, March 16, 2008
(Palo Alto)
There have been a few major changes the last few days.

David has starting whispering single words, though he must usually be prompted. For instance, if you are giving him something to eat or drink, and you ask him if he wants "more", he will whisper the word "more". Sometimes it is little more than mouthing the word.

He will sit and do his voice exercises on his own. It is a bit like clearing his throat. He is sounding stronger and clearer by the day.

Some of the words that he's speaking when prompted include "hi, stop, more, Dad, Sem, no, David". He's having trouble with "yes" and "Mom", but he does try.

He hasn't said "hi, Dad" yet, but Sem did prompt him to say "hi" and then prompted him to say "Dad". She knows that I'm waiting for him to say "Hi, Dad" when I come into his room. He hasn't done that yet, but I know that it's coming. Maybe this morning.

During his physical therapy yesterday, one of the therapists was giving him something to drink. When she gave him more, and then more, I stopped her and said she should ask him first, then I asked him. He said "more" and it was clear and it was well above a whisper. Looks like David may be coming back.

Then, last night after Sylvia and I left David and returned to our hotel, David did a little more than whisper a word. Sem and the nurse were getting him ready to put him in the lift in order to set him in his shower chair and take him into the shower. As you know, he doesn't like the lift very much. So when he saw them wheel it over, he whispered rather distinctly "I hate that f***ing thing". It was a harsh whisper, but Sem says that she understood every word. She called us immediately to tell us.

I have also noticed that David is responding to commands very well. When asked to do something, he understands and does it quickly (well, so long as he is willing). "Lean forward, take a deep breath, open your mouth".

Another important item... David's sweating appears to be gone. He has been having a problem with his feet sweating for months. We were told at Walter Reed that this is very common with brain injury patients. To see the sweating stop so suddenly has to be a good sign.

Sylvia got permission to feed David. For lunch yesterday he had Chinese food take out. We all sat around the table in the Day Room and had lunch together. He's having absolutely no trouble eating. He even laughed and chuckled now and then as we talked around the table. Important thing here is that he didn't choke.

David and I spent several hours on our own yesterday afternoon. He had had a very busy morning and needed to rest. He was awake most of that time, eyes open and he appeared to be in thought. During that time, I noticed that whenever someone came into the room, he closed his eyes. It seems clear to me that he is using this as a way not to be bothered. We suspected that he was doing this during the night (they said he was sleeping thru the night, but we didn't think so), and I think this is evidence that we were right.

We're getting ready to head over to the trauma unit.

Monday, March 17, 2008
(Palo Alto)
David was less vocal yesterday (Sunday) than Saturday, but he did say "yes" several times, and he was having trouble with that word before.

He also did something that is really important. In the past, David's only unprompted words have been his colorful, emotionally charged words. Yesterday, he spoke his first unprompted request.

Sylvia made a turkey dinner last night. We were all in the Day Room having dinner together. David got a little impatient for his next bite, so he said "more" to Sem.

We've been working on this word, sometimes when he is being fed, more often when given juice or ice tea. He will be asked "more?", and if he says more will get another sip of juice or a bite of food. (Sometimes he will say or mouth the word, other times simply nod.)

His words are still whispers, and except for those very rare occasions they are single words and only when prompted, but he is beginning to communicate. When he says the word, he usually means it. No means no, yes means yes, and when he says more he means he wants more.

In PT yesterday they put him on the bicycle. This is the apparatus where he remains in his wheelchair and the therapist places his feet on the pedals and turns on the machine.

The therapist set the speed to very slow. He encouraged David to push on his own. The machine monitors whether it is doing the work or David is actually pedaling and with how much effort.

David would struggle for a few moments, then put on his most menacing grimace and begin pedaling. He would go all out for several seconds at a time, the therapist urging him on, watching the readings and telling David what he was seeing. David would have to stop and let the machine take over, then after a bit he would take off again.

The therapist said "so you're a sprinter rather than a marathoner".

As David worked the bicycle, the therapist encouraged him to look at the numbers on the panel so that he could see for himself what he was doing. When David was really going, Mitch showed him that he was "breaking his old speed record". If anything is going to get David going, it's tapping into his competitiveness.

I think that David is gaining greater and greater understanding of what is going on around him, but we really won't know for sure what he is really comprehending until he is better able to communicate with us. For the moment, that communication is limited to his most immediate wishes, and then for the most part only when we prompt him.

But I am seeing really exciting progress these past few days, physically and cognitively. His progress comes in spurts and who knows how far this current spurt will take him?

With some of the other soldiers here, when they began speaking it always seemed to come in a rush. One day there was nothing, the next day they were having long conversations with their families. David's injuries were more widespread than many, and all brain trauma is unique to the individual. David's recovery has been <u>much</u> more slow paced and drawn out. There is always the fear that what we see today or tomorrow or the next day will be as far as David will go. We are warned of this possibility, and try to brace ourselves for it. Yet we also see and hear how encouraged all the therapists are by what they are seeing.

Who knows what I'll see when I go to his room this morning?

Tuesday, March 18, 2008
 (Palo Alto)
(morning)
David made more progress yesterday.

At the beginning of his speech therapy, the therapist asked
David what his last name was, and David whispered
"Beshears". She then asked him what his middle name was,
and he whispered "Michael".

She didn't say the names beforehand. He didn't just repeat
words back. He understood the questions, knew the answers,
and responded. Also, these are both multi-syllable words.

During the session, the therapist held up objects, asked David
what they were, and he answered correctly to "scissors", "ball",
and "brush". Again, they were hushed whispers, but they were
very understandable responses. He was uncertain about the
cup, but I think this may have been because he thought she
was asking him what was in the cup.

She placed the ball in his hand and asked David to show her
how you use it. He made a slight movement that we construed
as throwing it. She placed the brush in his hand and asked him
again and he made a slight brushing stroke.

In the evening, our family took a walk around the hospital
grounds. We were talking, and I said "no, no, no" to a comment
Sem made: "okay, you men can go camping, and we women
will go shopping in New York". My grandson and I like camping,
and David likes camping. I'm afraid Sylvia and Sem are less
inclined to such activity. (No, it isn't because of the work. As
camping is my idea, I usually get to do all the camping chores).

David was listening to us and picked up on my "no, no, no". He
apparently liked the sound of it. He said "no, no, no". He spoke
well above a whisper and said it with the same inflection I had
used. He liked the sound of his voice and so he said it again..
And again...

I don't know whether he was also joining in on the
conversation (he is very interested in surrounding
conversations, and I always try to include him). He may have

been trying to add his own comment to the "we women go to New York" idea, but it is important that David spoke in a normal voice. The therapist has been trying to get David to take a deep breath and breathe out when he speaks in an effort to get him to speak in a normal voice, and has given him exercises to do this.

David has been showing cognitive progress almost daily since the end of last week. He's not holding conversations, seldom speaks more than a single word and (almost) always needs to be prompted, but he does appear to be improving, and doing so quickly. He will get frustrated and agitated, will begin whispering "yes" to every question just to get you to leave him alone. He can also become very childlike in his manner.

He will also get angry and begin cussing. An interesting thing here, though. He has become angry and impatient with me, but has not cussed at me. I've heard him cuss up a storm at everyone else, but with Dad he just makes an angry face. At least so far...

He is still using "closed eyes, don't bother me" in attempts to be left alone. He uses this with everyone, and he does this whether he is in his bed or his wheelchair.

He did this again during occupational therapy yesterday, but when they asked me to work with him, he opened his eyes and we managed some activity. We had tug-of-war, arm wrestling, and pushed a large ball back and forth. David's arm constrictions are still very prevalent. I do have real concerns here.

An observation that several of us have made independently... we have been getting the impression that David's mind has become so active, his brain has begun processing so much incoming data, that he becomes frustrated and agitated by all the incoming "noise". We have asked everyone to be much more careful about holding only one conversation at a time, to keep talking to a minimum when he's watching television, and so on. These are things the therapist asked in the past, and they now seem to be much more relevant. We have come to an important milestone in David's recovery.

During our dinner last night in the Day Room, we found that David was more relaxed and seemed to enjoy the "calm" conversation. He laughed several times at memories and not just the words. We were talking about his dogs and when his kids would mention one antic or another, I saw David's face light up and he would laugh lightly.

During our walk after dinner, we again tried to not talk over one another. David was quiet through most of it, but appeared attentive, more relaxed, and of course spoke up with his "no, no, no" during our camping conversation.

Enough of my ramblings for this morning. I'm going to get ready to head over to the tbi unit.

Tuesday, March 18, 2008
Palo Alto (evening)
David continued to show progress today. During his speech therapy he said (harsh whisper) his full name when asked. When asked how many children he had, he mumbled "one boy one girl". He named his children.

During pool therapy he "walked", with the help of a therapist in front of him, a therapist behind him, and being assisted forward. You could see him lifting his feet and bending his knees.

He is speaking in a normal voice now almost as much as he whispers. He is stringing a lot of words together, though it is often difficult figuring out what he's saying.

He will quickly repeat back words that you tell him, and once he's gotten a sentence down, he will often say it in a normal voice: "Want more orange juice".

Today he was even more frustrated and more easily aggravated than yesterday and in days past. I believe that much of this is due to his mind taking in so much that he is more easily overwhelmed. Also, it must be frustrating to be saying things and not being understood.

He really does need more quiet rest time alone to process all he's taking in, and when people are around, they need to be careful to have only one conversation going on at once.

And he really does like the sound of his voice... particularly in the pool building with all its echoing quality. There was a lot of loud "AHHHHH" going on in there...

He is still confused about many things. When given a choice about two things, he will often choose the wrong one. For instance, when asked if he is in a school or a hospital, he said "school".

Still, he is coming along very, very quickly. Each day seems so much more than the day before. Even though I fully expect there to be days with little obvious progress, I believe his brain will be continuing to heal itself during those slower times, and he will undoubtedly need those slow times.

Many of the medical and administrative staff around here are as excited as we are (perhaps they hadn't been as hopeful as we were). The last few days, since their staff meeting, many have come by to tell us how happy they are to hear of David's progress.

Sem says that she thinks David will be talking in a matter of days. She could be right, but I'm going to say it will be weeks and then be happy when it's days...

Thursday, March 20, 2008 (Palo Alto)
David has started having nightmares, flashbacks, and he imagines that there are "terrorists" around him. When he was "training" (working alongside) Afghani police, this is how they referred to the bad guys.

This started today after we left. Sem will tell him that he is safe, that he is in California, that there are no terrorists, but he insists they are there. The only way to calm him down is for Sem to call us and have David talk to his Mom and Dad. Listening to us on the phone helps. Perhaps it brings back the feeling of being safe at home that he had when he was young.

I wish we hadn't left.

Monday, March 24, 2008
(Palo Alto)
I spent almost an hour talking with David's doctor, and we went over just about everything.

Overall, he is very happy with the recent progress that David has made.

The doctor did finally acknowledge that David is a bit unique in his extremely slow, plodding progress through the stages of consciousness. It is because of this that it is very difficult to classify David. While he may be mostly in one level, he will also be partly in the one below, the one above, or both.

When David first fell into unconsciousness following the IED blast, he went into a full coma, level one on the Rancho scale. There are seven levels. Fully conscious (most of us, though perhaps not all...) can be considered level seven.

Throughout our time at Walter Reed, David was in level one and level two, "vegetative state".

He was mostly in two through his four weeks in ICU at Palo Alto, with only a few very minor indicators that he might move to level three, which is "minimally conscious".

After finally being transferred to the TBI unit, he began to move more into level three. I remember talking with the speech therapist after we had been in the unit for a few weeks. She told us that she considered him to be mostly in three, with one foot in level two and maybe showing a few indicators of level four (I think she was throwing us a lifeline with this).

Level four is "no impairment to consciousness".

The doctor told me that he now considers David to have "no impairment to consciousness". So, this would place him squarely into level four.

Most TBI patients move through the stages rather quickly, and it is easy to identify what stage they are moving through in any given week. But David is "drawing it out very slowly", and always has one foot in the stage behind while leaning forward toward the next stage.

From some of the doctor's notes that I've seen, I think the doctors had grown very doubtful that David would progress much further than where he was a couple of weeks ago.

Now, though, it is all up in the air again. Level four seems to me to be a real jumping off point.

David is going through a period where he will often be extremely confused, will say the most bizarre things, will focus on one word and repeat it again and again. He has moments of anger, agitation, frustration, impatience. By the time you ask him what's bothering him, the moment will be past and he will be serene.

The doctor says that the nightmares and flashbacks are unlikely to be from the IED blast. Most victims never remember the time leading up to or following the incident. More likely, David is recalling the months before. That doesn't help any... these kids are going through awful experiences over there for months on end.

He believes these flashbacks will happen over the next few months as David continues to progress. They commonly last a few seconds, and are much more traumatic for the family members than the patients. This is because for the patient once the moment is past everything is fine again, while for the family member the incident lingers on, and you are helpless to do anything about it.

Thursday, March 27, 2008
(Palo Alto)
David "calls" us almost every day.
Sem dials the phone and puts it on speaker so that David can talk to his mom and dad.

Today, he wanted Sem to call early. Actually, he was pretty emphatic about it.
So, she dialed and Sylvia just finished talking with him (I'm still at work...).

He said "Mom. I want beans."
Sylvia asked "You want me to make beans?"
David: "Yes."
Sylvia: "When we go down to see you, I'll make a pot of beans.
Okay?"
David: "Thank you."

(Sylvia makes really good beans. Her refried beans and
homemade tortillas are my favorite food.)

Sem says that David got mad at her earlier because he didn't
talk to us yesterday.
She says that she will see that David gets to talk with us every
day.

His speaking is slowly evolving into conversations. The words
are loud mumbles, and it sounds like he's "pushing" the words
out, but they are forming sentences that usually make sense,
and we can sometimes get exchanges going back and forth.

Sure looks to me like he's still moving up the consciousness
scale.

I'm looking forward to my next conversation with the speech
therapist.

Friday, March 28, 2008
(Palo Alto)
I just finished up a teleconference call with the staff at Palo
Alto (and staff up here at Ft. Lewis' Warrior Transition Brigade).

Medically, David is doing very well. The medical issues that he's
been dealing with these past months are resolved or are nearly
so.

Because of his ongoing physical issues, he is still on pain
medication. In addition to methadone three times a day, he is
taking oxycodone prior to physical therapy sessions.

David has increased Range of Motion in both his arms and his
legs, with continual improvement each week. However, he still

has quite abnormal tone (constriction) in his arms, so much so that his hands are not yet functional. Everyone is pretty much in agreement that this issue is the greatest concern. And it is a serious concern.

Occupational therapy also says that working with David on his arm constriction causes him quite a bit of pain. I see this every time I sit in on one of the sessions.

Of course, he is still not able to stand (or even sit, without support). His time in pool therapy is helping with this. David is doing better at making the proper "walking" movements while in the water. One of his legs, the one that wasn't injured, is doing much, much better than the other. He has problems controlling both, and can barely move the one.

The Occupational Therapist noted that David's "alertness" level has made huge advances these last few months. She says that when she first saw David in November, he was at a level 2 (on her 2-16 scale). He is now at a level 16. From her OT perspective, David has moved up from minimally conscious to conscious.

This corresponds somewhat with the diagnosis of other doctors and therapists, who have moved David up on their "Rancho" scale from level 3 to level 4, with signs of level 5. This scale has variations, and the one Palo Alto uses goes up to level 8. With all the Rancho scales, you can think of level 3 as minimally conscious and level 4 as "no impairment to consciousness". You still have a ways to go, you have serious consciousness issues, but the lights are on.

Today, the therapist held up a pen and asked what color it was. David told her. She then held up another pen of a different color and asked the color. David answered correctly.

Yesterday the speech therapist had David recite the alphabet. A couple of times she had to give him a bit of help, but he did make it through.

The next goal as regards "stages of consciousness" is for David to learn and then retain what he learns. This, in addition to managing agitation and confusion and so forth, will move David up to the next level.

And then there was this morning...

Sem was a bit late getting in to see David. She's been showing up at 9:00, what with dealing with the kids and all. At a little past nine, David started getting after the nurse to call Sem. "Call Semiha, call Semiha." I guess this nurse didn't know the number to call (it's right there on the wall). When Sem got in to see him at about 9:20, she heard about what had happened. She asked David about it. He said "nine, nine, nine."

Not only did David know to expect Sem in the morning, but he knows what time she comes in, he knew what time it was, and he knew that she was late.

Wednesday, March 02, 2008
(Palo Alto)
Some issues have come up regarding when David will be moved and to where.

Because David has effectively "emerged", he has graduated from the Emerging Consciousness program.

The goal has been to bring David far enough along that he could be moved up here to Washington with us.

Just a matter of weeks ago, the staff at Palo Alto had given the green light for David to stay in their program until June, when the kids will be getting out of school, and at that time determine which program would be best for David to move into. He would have been in the Emerging Consciousness program far beyond the normal schedule. As everyone knows, David has moved through the stages of consciousness extremely slowly.

Now, however, this has all changed. And no one knows where David will be cognitively from week to week. He continues to show improvement.

Now Palo Alto is arranging for David to be moved to a facility in Menlo Park in about three weeks. Sem and the kids would be able to stay at the Fisher House at the VA hospital until the kids finish school and Sem could drive to Menlo Park each day to be with David.

Once the kids get out of school, David would be moved up here to Washington State. The facility he would move to would depend on where David is cognitively at that time.

Sem is really upset. Moving a patient in David's condition always, always, always sets the patient back weeks. Especially if the transfer is done with a Medivac cargo jet. To move him in three weeks, and then move him again in June, would cause him tremendous trauma.

And we have to wonder about the other patients in the unit who have been there for months, who walk around on their own, eat in the Day room on their own, etc. I would point to them and say "whatever program they're in, put David in until June". Let's move him only once. A big concern for me is the "tone" in David's arms. His Occupational Therapist is working very hard to ease David's constriction.

I couldn't teleconference in on this last meeting.

Sem, rather than arguing with him, simply told them that if David couldn't stay where he was until June that she would rather pull the kids out and move David up to Washington. Then she said "you can deal with my Father-in-law", and that was the end of that.

So... I'm set to meet with them on Monday. I'm not sure where this will go, but I hope to have it resolved one way or another, and we'll at least know their reasoning behind their plans.

Monday, April 07, 2008
(Palo Alto)
David has been very agitated the last few days. H's quick to get upset and will refuse to do things. This is all a sign of the stage he's going thru (a primary indicator of level 4), but it can be as frustrating for us as it is for him.

He is speaking more and more, but what he says can often be wrong. He'll put together a complete sentence, and do it correctly, but it will be to tell you that your hair is blue.

David will pick up a word or phrase and then use it as an answer the rest of the day.

Again, this is all to be expected at this stage in his progress.

Next... Yesterday during his PT, David told his therapist that he wanted to walk. She hadn't asked him about it. He just indicated the hallway and then said that he wants to walk.

Today was OT (occupational therapy) day, to work on his arms, which he refused to do. He was very vocal about it. We'll see what he does at PT tomorrow...

We wheeled David over to the main hospital today to see an ENT (Ear, Nose and Throat doctor). We had to sit in the waiting room for almost an hour. We're all part of the same complex... And we're coming from a brain trauma unit... And they called to ask us to bring him over. So what's the deal?

 Next... The other day, the speech therapist asked David "When are your Mom and Dad coming down?" He said "Sunday". And she said that he looked happy and excited... I'm not sure what she means by that. David's emotional state these days seems to be contentment on the one hand, and frustration, agitation and anger on the other.

From what I've seen though, I think David will be moving through this stage relatively quickly. Not everything is firing yet, but I think he's fully self aware. You have to remind him where he is, and therapists have to prompt him as to who they are and why they're there. Remember what I said in an earlier email. David's next big cognitive hurtle is "to learn, and then retain what he learns".

I had a chance to talk with one of the doctors today about David's schedule, mostly regarding the issue of moving him right at the moment that he is progressing so well. He said that he was going to take this up with the administrator who makes final decisions on such matters. The staff is set to meet tomorrow.

On a lighter note, not long before we left David this evening, Sem, Sylvia and I were sitting with him in his room. Sem called the kids, who were over at the Fisher House, and put it on speaker phone. David talked with Ashley first, even said "Hello Ashley", and asked her how she was. He then said "talk to Kevin". Ashley put Kevin on. David asked "How are you doing?" Kevin responded "How are you doing?" David said "I asked you first".

So David asking "How are you doing" is more than just an autonomic response to talking with someone. He was asking the question and was listening for the response.

Many of David's questions and answers tend to fall into the autonomic category. He says something because at this point in a conversation, it is what you are supposed to say. But then, don't we all? Um... perhaps they mean more to David than they do to the rest of the world.

During the time that David was at Palo Alto, I usually sent status updates out each night after Sylvia and I returned to the hotel for the night. I would plug in the micro-PC that I bought just for these trips, write up the status update (hardly visible on the little 4 ½ inch screen) and send it off.

When we were at home during that time, between trips, I sent out status updates a bit less frequently, but still managed to get them out once or twice a week, as the news warranted. If I didn't, it wouldn't take long and I'd start hearing about it. Family would start calling, and friends (or people I knew only through the updates) would start sending emails wanting to make sure that everything was all right.

Tuesday, April 08, 2008
(Palo Alto)
David had speech therapy and pool therapy today. In speech, he worked primarily on expanding his diet. Lonna had him take bites of several different foods and tested his ability to swallow. During the session, she asked him questions about the date, where he was, how old he was, how old his kids were. I'm afraid he doesn't do well with these just yet.

Two other things that David needs to work on so far as the mechanics of speaking, and they are somewhat related.

When most people speak, they bring air up from their lungs. David uses only what air he happens to have in his mouth at the time. Because of this, his words sound mumbled and "pushed".

David also runs his words together. I think he does this because he knows he only has so much air to get through the sentence.

In pool therapy they worked on walking. He can sometimes get the leg movement right for one or two steps, so you can see that he understands what needs doing; he's almost there, but not quite. He also has a lot of difficulty straightening up to walk, and the therapists are working on this.

And finally... the medical staff got together today and came to a decision regarding David's schedule. They have agreed that David's discharge date will be June 12. This is great, because it will give him a chance to continue through this phase of his recovery before being moved.

By a weird coincidence, David's new discharge date, June 12, is the same as my discharge from the army (before you ask, it was 33 years ago).

Wednesday, April 09, 2008
(Palo Alto)
David had good sessions in physical therapy and in speech therapy today.

As good as they were, however, neither can compare to the ten minutes he spent with the recreational therapist and the dog she brought in to see him.

When the big black lab brought his front paws up onto the bed and looked expectantly at David, I watched a warm, glowing smile spread across David's face. He was genuinely happy.

The therapist put a small doggie treat between David's thumb and finger. David's arm moved slightly as he tried to give the treat to the dog, and he grinned when the dog worked the treat free, licking David's fingers.

The therapist told David that the dog should earn the next one. She asked David to have the dog sit. David said "sit" and the dog sat. David looked very pleased. The dog brought his front paws and head up onto the bed for the treat.

The therapist asked David if he would like to pet him. David said yes. He then managed to move his arm enough so that his hand touched the dog's head. David smiled again.

The therapist asked what David kind of dog he has. He said "black lab" (he does). She asked the dog's name. David said "Trixie".

The therapist and David spent several minutes on the subject of Trixie. David truly enjoyed the session.

Tuesday, April 15, 2008
(Palo Alto)
David is now officially on a "normal diet". This means that he chews and swallows well enough that the staff is confident that he will not choke or swallow the wrong way; he is able to eat any food. They still look in his mouth every few bites and he is given something to drink after a few bites. He is still not able to

use his hands, so either Sem or one of the nurses has to feed him.

David still has the stomach peg, as this is still being used to give him one of his medications. Several pills they have been crushing and mixing into pudding and feeding to him, but there is one that would cause serious side effects if it was exposed to the mouth. A few days ago the medical staff began giving him some of his pills orally in whole form, testing whether or not he will consistently swallow without chewing the pills. He needs to understand the difference between food and medicine, every single time. Once they are confident that he won't bite down on pills, they will begin giving him this last pill orally. Once he's done this for a while without incident, they will remove the stomach peg.

David is being exposed to public settings more and more. He's taking this better as the days go by, but still needs his quiet time, before and after each therapy and after spending time in any sort of public setting.

He still can't use his hands or arms. He is also unable to sit or stand without support. He did, however, manage to sit on the edge of the raised platform for 1 minute, 50 seconds before the therapist had to take hold of him. What they are looking for is David's ability to use various stomach and back muscles to correct himself as he begins to fall forward, backward or to the side.

David has not yet crossed the threshold of "learning and retaining what he learns". If you tell him the date, and then two minutes later ask him the date, you're not going to get the correct answer. He will usually give you some sort of "date information", but it won't be the date that you just told him. He may just throw out any date, or he may give you a string of months all pushed together ("JanuaryFebruaryMarchAprilMay"). He will understand the subject of date, but not how it applies, and he won't have processed and stored the date that you just gave him.

He is also told daily where he is, but if you ask him, he will usually say "I don't know" or give you an answer that is tied in to something that was being talked about earlier. For instance, if the subject of school or home came up earlier, he may say "home" or "school" He understands the concept of location, but cannot as yet retain the knowledge that he is in the hospital.

However, there may be some progress here. The other day he was told that he was in the "hospital in Palo Alto, California". A few minutes later, when asked, he said "hospital in Palo Alto California". It was a repeated back word for word statement, with the same inflection, but it was an accurate response to what was asked. A definite step forward. But a few minutes later, when asked again, it was back to "I don't know".

The plan is still to bring David up here to Washington in June. I will probably be taking three more trips down to Palo Alto, the third trip to bring the grandkids up as David and Sem fly up on the Medivac.

We have been told that where David is transferred will be our choice. Palo Alto will be sending feelers out to facilities up here in the Northwest. Once they get responses back, these will be presented to us and we can say yea or nay.

Sylvia and I have already begun looking around on our own. While it would be great to find some place close, some place near Olympia, we will choose the best location for David. It needs to be the best brain trauma facility, with an equally highly regarded physical / occupational therapy program. If two places are equally good, we would choose the one further south. As of now, we can find nothing outside Seattle.

We are very much open to any input that any of you have on this. It must be "recovery and rehab", not "storage". It must have a strong physical / occupational rehab program as well as cognitive recovery. If you know of any facility that might be worth looking into, or, just as importantly, that we should steer clear of, please let me know.

Wednesday, April 16, 2008
(Palo Alto)
David gave us a really big surprise a little while ago, and I really
need to tell everybody...

I sent an email to Sylvia telling her about the Good Samaritan
hospital in Puyallup, a place that several of you told me about. I
mentioned in the email that we should look into the program
there and see if it's something that would be good to put David
into.

Sylvia called Sem to tell her about it. She told her that it wasn't
too far from where they had planned to move to once David
retired from the Army.

Sem was with David when Sylvia called, and she had the call on
speaker.

Sem asked Sylvia "How far is Puyallup from you guys?"

Before Sylvia could answer, David said "About an hour".

I don't know, but this seems really, really big to me...

Oh, and I did a Map Quest on the distance. The hospital is 57
miles from my house.

Cool, or what?

Monday, April 28, 2008
(Palo Alto)
Sylvia and I drove up to Good Samaritan hospital in Puyallup
this weekend to have a look at their Rehabilitation center. We
were really happy with what we found, and our first impression
is that it would be a great choice for David.

They appear to have very good physical and occupational
rehabilitation programs, perhaps even more extensive, more
structured and more organized than what he has in Palo Alto.
Palo Alto was excellent for the "emerging consciousness" stage
that David went through. I think Good Sam will be a good next
step.

We also found they have a "hand therapy" program devoted solely to helping David with his hands. I am really, really happy about that, and I will be looking more into this. As you know, I'm very concerned about the issue with David's hands.

The rehab center also has speech pathology, social integration programs and family involvement in the rehab process.

From what I saw, it looks like they go beyond just "learning to live with disability" and really aim at making the person better. We saw a number of subtle indications of this.

I know that some think that I'm in denial about David's condition, but that's not true. I just refuse to put limits on the possibilities while David continues to improve. I want David back and I'm going to do whatever it takes to give him the best possible opportunity to return as close to 100% as he can get. No, I won't put limits on expectations. If I do everything possible to create the opportunities, then he'll come back as far as he is physically and mentally capable of coming back, whatever those levels might be. I'll take what I can get, but I won't take any less. I'll do what I have to do so that he can do what he has to do.

On a lighter note...

Sylvia heard an interesting story from Sem yesterday. Apparently David has a new speech pathologist that works with him on the weekends. From what I can gather, she was working with him on grouping items in categories (asking him how things are similar?). At least, I think that's what it was about. I heard this second hand. So, the list included doctors, nurses, therapists... I'm not sure what answer she was expecting, but I understand that David responded "pains in the ass".

David's sense of humor is back.

Saturday, May 03, 2008
(Palo Alto)
We got into Palo Alto about 4:30 this afternoon. The trip went
fine until we reached the nightmare mish-mash of highways
down here. The more I drive around here, the more I reinforce
my desire to live in a small town outside Olympia.

We were worn out from the trip, but once we had checked into
our room and got settled in, we went over to the trauma unit
to see David for a few minutes. He knew we were coming
down, and Sylvia had talked to him when we were about four
hours out. Once he knew we had arrived, he wanted to see us.

David looks pretty good and he was talkative. However, he was
speaking in mumbles, much of which I really couldn't
understand. I did notice that he would often repeat back your
words when answering a question, and just put "yes" or "no" in
front of the sentence.

We were told that he has a UTI (urinary tract infection), so they
are starting him on antibiotics. Also, he will still "pocket" his
medications in his cheek, so for the time being the stomach peg
is going to stay in order to give them a way to get the one med
into him that can't be sprinkled into his food.

We'll be spending most of tomorrow with him. Monday we
meet with staff about David's moving up to the northwest.

Sunday, May 04, 2008
(Palo Alto)
David seemed really tired most of the day. He's on one of those
med cycles where they give him pills to perk him up and more
pills later to quiet him down. This is supposed to help his
concentration during his various therapies and then help him
sleep on a regular cycle at night.

They cut back his little pick-me-ups by half because they think it
may be contributing to his agitation. Unfortunately, between
this and the antibiotic they've started him on, the kid looks half
asleep.

Still, his mom and I had a very nice time with him at dinner. He and I watched the news while his mom fed him. Sem said that he has really been into the news lately, and insists that she put it on for him.

Sem was with Ashley much of the day, helping her get supplies for a school assignment, and then later staying with her at the Fisher House as she worked on it.

Ashley made a "four course dinner" for us, so after we got David settled in after his dinner, Sylvia and I walked across the street and joined Sem, Kevin and several other guests who are staying at the Fisher House as Ashley served us a great dinner, with Chicken Fettuccini as the main dish. I think she should get an A.

It's now Monday morning at 6 AM. We meet with staff today to discuss David's status and go over transfer options.

Tuesday, May 06, 2008
(Palo Alto)
We had our meeting with the staff down here yesterday and they are going to start working on placing David at the rehab center in Puyallup. They told us that from what we said it doesn't sound like it would be a problem. The facility must not have been on their current "short list" however, because the social worker had to have me write the word "Puyallup". She's obviously not from the Northwest...

If the arrangements can be made and the rehab center has a bed ready for him (it looked like it from what Sylvia and I saw) then David's transfer should happen around the weekend of June 14-15.

The doctor talked to us about David's hands, and again brought up the possibility of surgery. First, though, there are a couple of things they can do that will give them more information. These procedures will temporarily "turn off the switches" and allow the muscles to relax. This will let the doctors know if the problem is muscles or tendons or even something else.

David worked with the full spectrum of therapists yesterday. I thought he did really well in each of them, and certainly much better than the day before.

His speech pathologist will often perform occupational therapy activities as a way of getting David into conversation and to test actions such as swallowing. Yesterday she placed a cup of ice in David's hand and worked with him to lift it to his mouth. It was just a little bit of an effort to get the cup and his hand in the right position, but once in place, he did lift it to his mouth several times, and she even got him to "shake the cup" to get ice to move into his mouth. She had to help a bit with the shaking part, but he did it.

The recreational therapist came in the afternoon. As she was getting a notebook out, she told David that she wanted to play a game of "football city". She was going to name a city, and she wanted David to name the football team.

I sat on the edge of my chair for this one...

She began naming cities...

Even before she would get the name all the way out of her mouth, he would mumble the name of the team.

He was looking intently at her, waiting patiently for her to name the next city.

I don't think she was ready for him to get them all. She was scribbling in her notebook. She looked over at me. "I'm running out of cities." So I started naming some that she had missed.

David got every one.

He really likes Rebecca's visits because as the recreational therapist, everything she does is in the form of a game. Also, she is the one who brings in the man with the dog.

When she has David choose colors or numbers, it's the game of Uno. She tells him that a certain card is on the discard pile, then holds up several cards and asks him which card he would play next. She even makes him use his hands to point (as best he can) to the card.

She sings songs with him. She will start a sentence, and he has to finish it.

They sang three songs yesterday. He did best with the first one. After they finished the third one, Rebecca told David it "looks like Sunshine is our best song" (You Are My Sunshine), David looked at her with the hint of a smirk and said "song sucks".

David has said to me several times that he wants to go home. His nurse and I got him ready to go to the gym yesterday and once he was all set, I said "okay, I think you're ready to go." Of course, he said "ready to go home."

He will look me in the eye and say "want to go home".

For him, home is Washington. He wants to go home to Washington. I've let him know that it's not going to be tomorrow, but that it's only a few weeks now. Now that he's ready, we're getting everything else ready, and as soon as the kids are out of school, he's coming home.

The speech pathologist told me that she sees a change in David several days before his mom and I come down. He's happier. And he's always a bit down for a few days after we leave.

She uses our arrival day as a way of building conversation with David. "What day are your parents coming down? Are they coming Wednesday or Thursday?" When we're here, she will ask him how many days we're staying.

Yesterday was a very busy day for David, and he didn't get much opportunity for his quiet rest time. By the end of the evening, he was getting pretty agitated. As we were getting him settled into bed, he even got short with me, and he's never done that. I couldn't understand what he was saying, but he was clearly letting me know that he was upset. We didn't want to leave him laying there stewing in the dark, so we turned the TV onto one of the light comedies (I think it was Family Guy, the one with the talking dog). He seemed happy with that.

Thursday, May 08, 2008
(Palo Alto)
David's pool therapy is focusing on deep knee bends. In this last
session, he started out slow but ended strong. One of the
therapists made a comment that really turned it into a bit of a
competition, and David is very competitive. It lit a spark
somewhere. He did good, and he actually looked like he was
enjoying himself. It was very cool.

The strategy is to carry whatever they do in the pool over to
the gym. If they can get David to use his legs, and especially his
knees, then they will be able to "transfer" David from bed to
wheelchair or wheelchair to gym equipment without having to
use the Hoyer lift. The lift is a time consuming, labor intensive
process, and it is stressful for David.

This would also be a very positive next step in David's physical
rehabilitation. He can't get on his feet if he can't stand up.

Another bit of news. David's stomach peg was finally removed
yesterday. He's had that i
n his belly since last October. So, hey, another milestone. Let's
keep them coming.

In other areas, it's still slow. I see some signs that give me hope,
but sometimes when I'm with David and things are quiet and I
have time to think, all the bad things we see every day come
creeping in and I have a really hard time putting on the
confident face. I get physically numb and sometimes feel sick.

Of course, then the speech pathologist comes in and asks David
if he's happy his parents are here and David says "Parents
great, parents great. Safe. Safe."

And I get really, really choked up.

Yesterday I told David I was going to have to leave, but that I
was going to finish getting everything ready to bring him home.
He said "Go Puyallup".

So while he will usually just repeat back what you say to him,
he does sometimes take in what you say and think about what
it means and respond with his own thoughts to your comment.

Little things like that keep us going. It gives me the strength to
fight back against placing limits on where he will end up.

Thursday, May 15, 2008
(Palo Alto)
I've put in quite a few hours since last Friday trying to figure a
way to get David into the rehab center at Good Sam.

Apparently, the quite extensive facility is designed to get
patients through inpatient status in two weeks and then push
them to outpatient status. While David has made progress, I
am not confident that he would be ready in such a brief time.
He was in a "vegetative state" for four months, and has only
been above "minimally conscious" for a matter of weeks. He
still needs a Hoyer lift to be transferred from bed to
wheelchair.

He has less than a month before we are to bring him up. A lot
can happen in that time, as we have seen. During my trip down
last week, the therapists had begun work trying to get David
away from needing the Hoyer lift. He will need to be able to
use his knees and legs at least well enough to provide some
support when being lifted from bed to wheelchair or the other
way around.

However, we've been told that David has been very agitated
the last few days. He is refusing to work with the therapists and
has been angrily ordering Sem out of the room. Sem will stand
at the door, out of view, and says she can hear him grumbling
angrily even when he is alone.

I hope this has nothing to do with Sylvia and I returning home
last week. I think it may very well be ongoing progress. The
head doctor of the brain trauma unit has told me several times
(and I've read this as well) that severe brain trauma patients
progress through a consciousness level in which they can
become extremely agitated.

We had believed David had already moved through this stage,
but as we know he has been very unique in how many levels he
has straddled at once.

In any event, we've been talking with the rehab center up here and David's case worker in Palo Alto. Nothing has yet been decided, but it is now not certain that he will be coming to Puyallup.

Friday, May 23, 2008
(Palo Alto)
We were supposed to be going to down to Palo Alto, but have yet to get out of town. I'm still hoping... maybe tomorrow...

I've been meeting with staff at rehab facilities all over the northwest for the last few days, and have yet to get the matter resolved as to where David is going to be staying once we bring him up in a few weeks.

I've also had two teleconferences with Palo Alto staff over the last two days, and have had numerous individual phone calls with our case worker.

It's pretty obvious now that most of the level 1 trauma rehab facilities have inpatient programs limited to 10 - 21 days, after which the patient moves to outpatient status. It really doesn't make much sense to me, not when you have a patient with severe brain trauma and multiple spinal injuries, but...

We've now been looking at bringing David into a "sub-acute rehab" facility and then supplement the provided therapy. It's even more difficult identifying the right place for David at this level, since the majority tend to be senior nursing homes with rehab as part of their services. I'm having a tough time finding a suitable place, though there have been several with nice rehab therapy rooms (but of course the staff are targeting our senior citizens). One administrator wondered how David would respond with everyone around him fifty years older than he is.

In the meantime, David's main doctor in Palo Alto is going to be doing a doctor-to-doctor conference with Good Samaritan's Rehab Center today to discuss David's unique situation.

As for David...

His attending physician brought in some famous bigwig hand surgeon for a consult on the constriction that is preventing David from using his hands. The doctor recommended holding off on the surgery (to cut David's muscles/tendons). He said that he believes David may still improve, and holding off for six months wouldn't hurt.

David continues to tell everyone that he wants to come home. When he's told that he will be going home in a couple of weeks, he says "Don't want to wait. Want to go home now".

David is starting to improve on moving his legs. Much of his therapy is focusing on strengthening and controlling his legs, with a lot of the emphasis on bearing his weight, all with an eye toward David assisting in his transfer from bed to wheelchair.

I have another visit to a facility just a few miles away in a few minutes, and I have one more call in to Palo Alto late this afternoon. Hoping to know more, then...

Wednesday, June 04, 2008
(Palo Alto)
I continue to work to bring David up from Palo Alto. There has been some progress, and I expect to see some finalization by the end of the week.

Good Samaritan is back in the picture. There has been discussion back and forth between David's head doctor in Palo Alto and the staff at Good Sam. It is very likely that I will be placing David there, though his length of stay is still up in the air. I will be talking with them again today, and conferencing with Palo Alto.

It is also very likely that when David leaves Good Sam, whenever that is, that he will be staying with us, in the house he grew up in, probably through the summer; at least that's the plan. If so, then we will become his "sub-acute" rehab facility. We have an exercise room, a 6' x 6' shower room, an extra-wide hallway, French doors that open out onto a 12' x 80' covered deck, swimming pool with surrounding deck at water level. Sylvia has been a med tech at a retirement center for 20+ years, and his sister and her husband have worked in the past as home health-care providers (mostly as sit-ins to give families a break from caring for elderly parents).

I need to finish adapting the home to care for David and buy any additional exercise / therapy equipment we need. We would have a therapist come in regularly and oversee his ongoing therapy program, nursing to come in to oversee medical needs.

This would give Sem time to take care of the remaining issues in Oklahoma (they still have a house there) and get set up back here in the Northwest.

I go down to Palo Alto next week to bring the kids up. They will be staying with us for a while, whatever happens with David.

David appears to be moving beyond the "very agitated" stage that he's been in for the past few weeks. Also, they've been putting him on the exercise bicycle but not turning on the power. He's been doing 100% of the work, and even using his hands in coordination with his feet. The physical therapist told me she was surprised at how well he's been doing with this.

David continues to mumble when he talks, and it isn't always clear what he's trying to say or even whether it makes sense, particularly when he becomes frustrated or over-stimulated. I do see signs of continuing progress, though it is painfully slow.

One item here; a couple of days ago he told Sem "I get confused". I interpret his statement this way. For him to understand that he gets confused, he has moments of clarity, and I believe that clarity is becoming more the norm than the exception.

Oh... and he wants to buy a boat.

Wednesday, June 04, 2008
(Palu Alto)
(evening)

I've been talking with Good Sam and Palo Alto, and here's the way things look...

Good Sam rehab is going to take David into their program. They say that he will be able to stay in their inpatient program "so long as there is progress". Where have I heard that before??? I told them that I would never let David stay anywhere that he wasn't making progress.

The admissions director said that in looking at David's status and progress, she believes David is "very appropriate" for their program. This is good. Their intensive program is designed to get patients through quickly and out to outpatient. If they think David is ready for them, they're seeing possibilities in David's prognosis.

Sylvia and I are going down to Palo Alto on Thursday, June 12. We'll be bringing the kids up on Saturday. David will be taken from Palo Alto by ambulance up to the nearby Air Force base on Sunday, June 15, and will be flown by Medivac up here on Monday, June 16th.

The kids will probably stay with us for a couple of months.

When David does leave Good Sam rehab, he will be coming to stay with Sylvia and me until Sem has a house set up for him. While with us, David will be continuing his physical rehab. Once with Sem, he will be part of an outpatient rehab.

The primary purpose of our tenth and final trip to Palo Alto was to bring Ashley and Kevin back up with us. Sem was going to be making the trip north in the medivac with David. With his rising level of consciousness, this was really important.

So we packed the back of the car tight with the kids' stuff, as well as most of Sem's, and at about 4:00 in the morning started out of Palo Alto for the last time. We hoped to see David and Sem in Puyallup in a few days.

The drive north from Palo Alto California to Olympia, Washington has a number of stages.

Sylvia and I usually left early enough in the morning that we could be well away from the Bay area before the traffic got bad. I always visualized it as a nightmarish web that spidered out from Oakland and reached out for a hundred miles in every direction.

So this meant that we drove the first few hours and reached I-5 in the Central Valley in the dark. There's a rest stop just after the interchange onto I-5 where we always stopped and took our first break.

Now this was to be the first trip with the grandkids. So far, so good; they handled the first leg of the road trip just fine.

The next few hours up I-5, the second leg in the trip, can be a bit boring. There is usually very little to see in the north Central Valley, even after the sun comes up. It's not that it's bad, but there's just not much there, though on this last trip there was one of the more spectacular sunrises that I've seen. There had been several wildfires in Northern California, and Sylvia and I had driven through heavy smoke on our way down. We had spent the night in a hotel where a number of firefighting crews were staying.

On the return trip, the smoke in the air made for a fantastic sunrise. For the kids, not really that exciting. I guess I'm easier to please.

The next stage in the drive is where we come up out of the valley, starting with the drive past Mt. Shasta, on into Oregon, then over the Siskiyous summit. I pointed out some of the really cool things to see, and Kevin took some pictures using his cell phone. I'm pretty sure that he sent some of them to his mom.

I always really liked the next stage of the trip; the drive from the summit down into the Willamette Valley is beautiful; some really gorgeous country. Sylvia and I have talked about spending some time there one of these days. We stopped at most of the rest stops so the kids could get a look at it.

The next stretch was where I think I may have lost the kids for good (figuratively, not literally). We were getting into the afternoon then, had been on the road since 4:00 in the morning and, well to be honest the drive up the Willamette Valley can get rather dull. We're out of the mountains now, and are traveling up the heart of the valley. A lot of little towns, one after another, mostly the same when seen from the highway, the route sprinkled with brief stretches of nature.

The worst, though, especially for the driver, starts about an hour or so south of Portland. The traffic starts getting congested, and will only get worse as we approach afternoon rush hour.

What's worse yet, from this point on to the Washington border there's nothing to look at. It's all buildings and freeway and traffic.

By the time we hit Portland itself, we've been on the road eleven or twelve hours. And we're likely to be at a dead stop on the freeway; just us and a few thousand of our closest friends.

It gets better at the next stage, and knowing this does make the Portland mess easier to put up with, at least from the driver's perspective.

We cross the Columbia River and enter Washington State. Sylvia and I always start to feel better here, because we have this sense of being home. And the scenery gets better. There's a lot more nature on either side of the freeway. It all seems so much fresher. And I think the rest stops are nicer. They're cleaner, anyway. Oregon may have better settings for some of their rest stops, but they're not as well maintained. California and Washington both have much cleaner rest stops than Oregon. With such beautiful, park-like rest areas, it's a shame that Oregon doesn't take better care of them. Oh, the smells I've smelled…

By this time, though, the kids just wanted it to be over. Please let it be over. But we still had at least a couple of hours to go. It's about a hundred miles to Olympia, and another half hour beyond that before we reach home.

All in all, I don't think they were as impressed with the road trip as me.

Tuesday, June 17, 2008
(Palo Alto)
We now have David's kids with us.

We drove down to Palo Alto on Thursday and Friday, drove back Saturday.

On the way down, traveling through northern California, we saw massive smoke plumes in the hills to either side of us. Staying in a hotel in Corning Thursday night, we found there were more than a few fire crews there with us. The next day, we passed dozens of fire crew trucks and emergency vehicles coming north to meet us.

On the way home Saturday, most the valley was in an ugly haze… absolutely beautiful sunrise, though.

We met with Palo Alto staff Friday afternoon for the final meeting. It served as a kind of hand-off. A number of them got a bit emotional. They've grown very close to David, and with us.

They all believe David is ready for this. Most repeated that what David really needs now, as much as his continued therapy, is to be close to his Mom and Dad.

The speech therapist told me that she wishes David was speaking as well as he was two weeks ago. She says that once he was told he was going home, he was pretty much done with Palo Alto. Every morning he wakes up wanting to know why he's not home.

They each gave Sylvia and me a hug, then handed me their cards and asked me if I could start sending them email updates and pictures.

David left Palo Alto on Sunday by ambulance, and was to spend Sunday night at Travis Air Force base, then fly up Medivac on Monday. Well... he and Sem did make it to Travis, but didn't fly up here yesterday. Now they're saying he'll be flying up this afternoon.

Kevin and Ashley are getting settled in with us. We're not quite ready to leave Kevin alone. They've both had to deal with an awful lot, and Kevin is really a bit younger than his years. I was off yesterday, and Sylvia is going to take off today and tomorrow.

We hope to be settling David into his new digs at Good Sam this afternoon.

Puyallup

Wednesday, June 18, 2008
(Puyallup)
David didn't handle the trip up as well as we had hoped. The
flight (a day later than planned, so David spent an extra night at
an Air Force base), was as noisy and stressful as any Medivac.
Once he got to McChord, there was no liaison to meet them.
An ambulance arrived and took David and Sem to Good Sam.
Sem felt completely lost and alone, David was stressed, tired,
bewildered, and found himself in a much smaller room than he
had before, sharing with another patient, with a view of a
parking lot rather than green lawns, trees, and the Fisher
House where his wife and kids had been living. This isn't home.

I got a phone call not long after they got David in his room. He
wasn't doing well. I immediately drove up. When I walked into
his room, David broke into a really big grin. With that, Sem
smiled and asked David "Are you happy?" David said "Happy.
Happy."

Sem seemed pretty glad to have someone there, too. The
paperwork got taken care of. We found where everything was.
David had dinner.

But, David started getting agitated again. He was still really tired, and now he also knew that he was going to have at least a few weeks at Good Sam. He had been told all along that he was going to Good Samaritan, to Puyallup, and he had been okay with that. He knew he was going to "Washington", and that he would "rehab" for a while. It was still going to be a while before he would be living with his family.

The rough trip and the realization that he was in another hospital made for a difficult experience.

I stayed there pretty late, then got Sem settled into a nearby hotel.

All the while, back home, Kevin spent the day wanting to know when Grandpa was coming home. His grandma kept telling him it would be 5:30, but he kept asking. Then he would ask "why so long?" and a lot of other questions you would expect of a much younger child. He's had a really difficult time, and it's going to take a while... Then of course they get a phone call from Good Sam and find out things aren't going so well there and their mom and dad are both having a time, and grandpa is going up there but that means he's not coming home...

Still, I think that once David gets used to his new surroundings, gets through the appraisal process and gets into his program, that things will turn around and we'll see some real progress.

At least the staff there has already seen a little of David's darker side.

This afternoon I'm picking up Sylvia and the kids and taking them up to Good Sam.

Monday, June 23, 2008
(Puyallup)
David seems to be settling in and I believe he is starting to do well at Good Sam.

Arms and legs all appear more limber, and he looks like he's moving them more naturally. He's sleeping in a regular hospital bed now and I've seen him adjust position to try to get comfortable if he's been in one position too long.

His cognition also seems to be a little better. He's consistently responsive and the responses are usually appropriate.

Some of things we've noticed:

His speech therapist asked him what year he was born and he said "1973". I think this is significant. When talking with him about dates, he will usually give answers that involve dates, but not always appropriate. You can lead him the answer and will often finish it, but this has been an area where he hasn't been able to retain very well, at least not consistently. Giving his correct year of birth without help is very good. I haven't heard of him doing this before.

His dietician came in with her computer to find out what David wanted for his three meals the following day. For each meal there were options for each course (main, side, drink, desert). She listed each option (i.e. Cheerios, Raisin Bran). David would wait until she finished the list, then give his answer. It was clearly what he actually wanted, and not just the first or last choice or a word that an interesting sound. She went through each item for each meal, and he let her know his wants for all meals the following day.

A friend of his from the military came in to see him for the first time. David knew who he was and responded to questions and comments pretty well (mumbling, but understandable). David held out his hand (shakily) to shake hands. David initiated it. When Dennis asked David what would be a good time to visit again, David said "five o'clock". This may have just been a time pulled out of the air, but it would be a time that is after his day's "work" of therapy sessions.

We spent the day with David yesterday (Sunday). At one point when things had quieted down some, David looked over at me and said "I'm happy".

Someone pointed to me and asked David "who's that?" David said "That's my Dad."

I put a bunch of photographs on the wall in his room and wheeled him over to the display. He studied the pictures, and after he had been looking at them a while, I asked him if he was through. He answered "not yet". So I let him look at them a bit longer.

His mom and I fed him his lunch yesterday (Sunday). When he was about finished, Sylvia pointed at a cookie and asked "would you like your cookie, now?" Instead of answering "yes", David reached over and tried to pick it up. Sylvia helped him get it into his hand and he began eating it on his own. He needed help a couple of times, but he's getting it. I saw on his daily schedule that he's getting "self-feeding" sessions each day.

We went into the Day Room and sat around a large, round table. Kevin got a ball (about the size of a volleyball), and we started rolling it back and forth to one another across the table. David tracked the movement of the ball 100% of the time (instead of looking in front of him and waiting for it to appear), and each time it came to him he adjusted the position of his hand and pushed the ball (using the back of his hand) in the direction of one of us. He used one hand for awhile, switched and used the other, then switched back. He did this a number of times. We played ball like this for about twenty minutes.

If David sees that two or three of us are just standing there staring at him, he'll look up at us and ask "what's wrong?". Natural response, if you ask me.

I don't think he gets as agitated quite as quickly as has the last few weeks, but he can get frustrated and he'll let you know it. If he's done eating and the aide or the nurse continues pointing to different foods to see if he wants this or that, after the third or fourth item he'll speak out quite clearly "I'M DONE!"

He does still say that he wants to go home. Also, once when Sylvia and I were spending time with him and we told him that we were going to go get something to eat while he rested for an hour in the afternoon, he let us know that he wanted us to come back. When we got back a little while later, he had rested and was ready to spend more time with us.

Things were really back and forth during David's time at Puyallup. Between his wanting to be home (he began emphasizing "home to McCleary") and the problems with medical staff, it just wasn't going to last long, no matter how hard everyone tried.

I really worked at putting the best possible light on it all, but in the end I had to relent.

The physical therapists did their best, even as David grew increasingly uncooperative. The floor medical staff, however, weren't used to dealing with someone in David's cognitive condition, and in several instances they were just plain negligent.

Tuesday, June 24, 2008
(Puyallup)
We've seen some progress with David since his arrival at Good Sam, but some serious issues have developed.

He seems to be benefitting from the physical therapy. He is more limber and his movements look just a little more natural.

As for cognition, he responds to his mom and me and the responses are consistently more appropriate.

When I am with him, or when Sylvia and I are with him, David does very well, is cheerful and interacts well with the staff at Good Sam. Unfortunately, when we're not there, David does not do well at all. He fights Sem, and he fights the staff.

When we're not there, Sem will call us and tell us to talk with David, to calm him down, tell him to take his pills, tell him to listen to her or the nurses, etc.

I go up there, and as soon as I walk into his room, he gets a big grin on his face and everything seems fine. He's looked over at me and said "I'm happy". He laughs when we talk with him. When his mom and I feed him, we've seen him reach for a cookie and try to eat it on his own (and he's getting better at this). We play games with him.

But he continues to say that he wants to go home. Sylvia and I are looking into this again. He needs to be home, and we'll bring the therapy program to us.

Monday, June 30, 2008
(Puyallup)
David continues to improve physically, albeit slowly, but I wish we would see a little more cognitively.
He's looking healthy; Skin color good, he's putting on a little weight, and as I have said before, his movements look more natural.

I know there's going to be ups and downs, good days and bad days, and days when nothing much happens, but lately he doesn't seem to be pushing the boundaries mentally. He continues to mumble when he talks (unless he's upset), to move his head from side to side when not focusing on something, and he still becomes agitated very easily.

Sylvia and I brought the kids up Sunday. Sem takes the kids out to the movies, restaurant and shopping each Sunday, while Sylvia and I spend the day with David. When we first came in, he wasn't in the best of moods. We did finally get him calmed down, and he did end up having a quiet enough day (Sunday is his day off from therapies), but he was never really fully "on". He would interact, but I didn't really see the sparks of sharper thinking that I've seen from him.

Christy (David's sister) and her husband also came up to spend a few hours. David knew who they were, would mumble sentences now and then, but it was like he was on the first step of a mental ladder and didn't want to step up one more. I've seen him on the next step, several steps higher actually, so I know he can do it.

I wish I could spend more time with him. Sylvia and I spend all of each Sunday with him, but it can be difficult to get up there during the week. We've managed a few trips midweek, but I think he would benefit if we were with him more. He seems to do better when we're there. Maybe the calming effect of his parents being with him allows his mind to better focus. I don't know...

From what Sylvia and I have seen, the staff at Good Sam are good with David, and very patient. The nursing staff all go out of their way to care for him, to look after him. No matter what their role, they interact with him in ways to encourage him to help himself, to think for himself. And during the therapy sessions that I've been present for, I've seen how the therapists work to move David towards doing things on his own. And that is the role of the rehab center.

So it's clear that David needs this time at Good Sam. Sylvia and I need to find a way to spend more time up there.

And Sem needs to get away for a while. She has her time away each evening (David goes to sleep pretty early these days), and she's coming in later in the mornings, but I think she needs to get away. It looks like she will soon. The military is still trying to get things sorted out regarding David's status (somehow, he's "attached" but not "assigned" to Fort Lewis). Once this is settled, Sem will be taking the kids to Oklahoma to get their house sold and what possessions they have there shipped to Fort Lewis.

Sem stepping away from David for a time may be good for David as well as Sem. You can see the affect of her moods in him. Sending in fresh(er) reinforcements may help them both. And, when she's back, she may have newly charged batteries. Again, good for them both.

Tuesday, July 01, 2008
(Puyallup)
We got a phone call from Sem yesterday (Monday). She said that David is saying (repeatedly) that he wants to "go home to McCleary". He wants to be with his Mom and Dad. I haven't told him that we've been looking into that. I would really like the rehab center have at least a few more weeks with him. I think the therapists are doing good things. I don't want his physical rehabilitation to come at the cost of his mental wellbeing, so we need to find the right time to move him and make sure that we can continue his physical therapy once we

get him home. In the meantime, Sylvia and I will do what we can to spend more time with him while he's at Good Sam.

Kevin and Ashley had their first Fourth of July with us. When David and his sister were young, Sylvia and I used to make quite a big deal out of the 4th, but since then, not so much.

But with the grandkids staying with us, we decided to do something, even if not quite as spectacular as in years past. So we took them down the fireworks stand and picked out a nice selection. The lady running the stand knew us, and knew of David, so we even got a discount.

Sem, staying with David, was a bit apprehensive about the kids being near fireworks. It didn't help matters much when, while talking to Ashley over the phone, Ashley described in blow-by-blow detail how grandpa was being assaulted by a spinner nailed to a post that had gone crazy, or later, also while on the phone with Ashley, when a firework that shoots fireballs into the air fell over and began shooting the balls of fiery death across the yard.

Tuesday, July 08, 2008
(Puyallup)
It looks like we're going to be bringing David home.

He continues to fight with the staff at Good Sam, and refuses to cooperate with the therapists. When I go up there and assist with the therapy sessions, he will work with them (grudgingly), but it all changes as soon as I leave.

He tells everyone "Want to go home – McCleary".

I've been talking with the staff the last few days. I think it's a done deal. We have a therapist coming out to have a look at the house and make recommendations. In the meantime, I've started on some things I know need to be done, and Sylvia and I are sorting out a schedule for ourselves.

The plan is to have David with us for a few months while Sem takes care of their house in Oklahoma and then gets settled in up here. We'll see where it goes from there.

Two of David's friends who were with him in Afghanistan came by to see him on Sunday when Sylvia and I were up there. David didn't show a lot of emotion, but you could see that he was glad to see them. They were good about bringing up the names of other soldiers they knew and telling David where they were now and what they were up to. They told some stories about incidents over there. I think it was a pretty good couple of hours for David.

Tuesday, July 15, 2008
(Puyallup)
I've been spending more time up at Good Sam with David this past week. While we're there, he's happy, he smiles, he laughs. When I work with them in his therapy sessions, he does extremely well and the therapists tell us the difference is night and day.

He was on the treadmill yesterday, hanging from a set of straps to keep him standing and keep pressure off his joints. He "walked" for nine minutes (There was a therapist on either side assisting him in lifting his feet). I stood in front of him and talked him through it, helped him focus, encouraged him to keep going. This was his first time on the treadmill and the therapists were very pleased with the session and are excited to try it again.

But when we're not there, David is unhappy, angry, agitated, and uncooperative. He won't work with the therapists and fights with the nursing staff. It's pretty much agreed by most now that he needs to come home.

The therapists have given us their recommendations on equipment and exercises. We're working with VA to get this stuff covered.

I go up to the rehab center on Thursday for a final day of training (therapy and general assist).

And I'm finishing up the modifications to the house. I probably won't have everything ready for him until next week, including installing the equipment, so the plan is to bring him home the following weekend.

One of the additional modifications I'm making to the house is putting in a set of French doors off David's room that open onto a small deck with a ramp (materials come in this week). This gives us direct access to his room from outside, and a view of the garden from his bed. I've already put in an archway between his room and the shower room.

The room David is going into was his bedroom growing up. He's really excited.

Thursday, July 17, 2008
(Puyallup)
We've been trying to spend more time up at Good Sam with David this past week.

While we're there, he's happy, he smiles, he laughs. When I work with them in his therapy sessions, he does very well and the therapists tell us the difference is night and day. This seems to be the case for all his therapies (speech, occupational, physical, recreational).

He was on the treadmill Monday, hanging from a set of straps to keep him standing and keep pressure off his joints. He "walked" for nine minutes (There was a therapist on either side assisting him in placing his feet). I stood in front of him and talked him through it, helped him focus, encouraged him to keep going. This was his first time on the treadmill and the therapists were very pleased with the session and are excited to try it again.

But when we're not there, David is unhappy, angry, agitated, and uncooperative. He won't work with the therapists and fights with the nursing staff. It's pretty much agreed by most now that he needs to come home.

The therapists are giving us their recommendations on equipment and exercises. We'll be working with VA to get this stuff covered.

We go up to the rehab center tomorrow for a final day of training (therapy and general assist).

And I'm finishing up the modifications to the house. We probably won't have everything ready for him until next week, including installing the equipment. We had hoped to bring him home on the 25th or 26th, but tonight I'm hearing that Good Sam would like to keep David until the 1st. Perhaps the therapists are seeing a change these past days and hope to build on that.

One of the additional modifications I'm making to the house is putting in a set of French doors off David's room that open onto a small deck with a ramp (materials come in this week). This gives us direct access to his room from outside, and a view of the garden from his bed. I'm finishing put in an archway between his room and the shower room.

The room David is going into was his bedroom growing up. He's really excited about coming home. He's even a little less uncooperative with the staff the last couple of days.

No matter how he's feeling, no matter what his mood, he needs to talk to his mom every day on the phone. He absolutely insists on it. It's just a couple of minutes, but I think it does him a lot of good. I know that Sylvia really likes it. David also had a conversation with Ashley the other day. She asked her dad if he remembered showing her how to make his favorite omelet. He said "yes". She asked if he remembered what he taught her to put into the omelet. David said "ham, egg and cheese". She asked "no bell pepper"? David said "no bell pepper. Ham, egg and cheese."

Tuesday, July 22, 2008
(Puyallup)
A lot of stuff going on right now.
I went through the training with each therapist on Thursday. As
I took David to each of his sessions, the therapist for that
session focused on what we will be doing with David once we
get him home.

We got the approval to have a therapist make house visits. We
didn't think there'd be a problem, but it's good to get the
official word. The therapist will be coming by a couple of times
a week to oversee David's therapies. No schedule set yet.

We got approved for Sem to get a wheelchair accessible
vehicle. We only get about 40% covered, and the vehicle isn't
cheap, but we'll be able to wheel David up to the front
passenger position. That's cool. She picks it up today.

We got prescriptions for the bed and the therapy equipment. I
had hoped to have it sooner. The stuff should be trickling in this
week.

As for the house preparations: I put in the French doors off the
room David that will be staying in. I had to rerun the wiring that
goes through that wall, so it took a bit longer. Got the room
painted. Still need to put in the trim. I finished putting in the
opening between his room and the shower, also did some refit
in the shower. I prepared the area outside the French doors to
ready it for the deck and ramp. I'll put that in on Thursday.

David comes home this weekend. Good thing, because he is
still fighting the staff at Good Sam. He wants to be home, is
very angry that he's not, and when he's told he's coming home
(they even point at the date on the calendar), he accuses
people of lying.

I'm developing a website for David. It's taking a little while,
since I'm writing it at night when I've finished with everything
else. I hope to have it ready by the end of the week. It will have
the latest status, status history, guestbook, background,
contact info page, etc.

Once the website is up, I'll send out the link. That will probably be the last status email I send out. Those interested in keeping an eye on David's progress (or would like to send him messages) will be able to go to the site anytime.

Thursday, July 31, 2008
(Puyallup)
David is coming home tomorrow.

He believes us now, and he's been growing more excited each day. He knows what day he's coming home, and he's been counting down the days with his mom. He's even less surly with the staff at Good Sam (some of this may be because they're backing off a bit).

The hospital bed arrives at the house today, finally. I was beginning to wonder. We're still waiting for most of the therapy equipment.

Sem's van arrived a few days ago, but is missing some part used to set the wheelchair in place (I think that's what it is. I'm not sure what they're talking about, I heard about this third-hand). If the van isn't ready by tomorrow, the army has reserved a wheelchair-accessible vehicle for us to transport David home.

The deck and ramp outside David's room is finished, excepting rails and detailing. This can wait until next week, after we have David settled in.

We had our home security company come out to the house yesterday and put a security sensor on the French doors. In addition to the regular alarm features, we set our system to chime each time the door opens when the system is not armed.

I'm putting some finishing touches on the projects around the house today, and we're getting everything organized, taking a close look at each room and making sure we haven't forgotten anything.

Also, there is some therapy equipment that I'm making by hand. I hope to have these ready over the next couple of days.

McCleary

Tuesday, August 05, 2008
(McCleary)
We've had David with us for a few days now. He came home Friday morning.

For the most part, he's very content. He does seem overly tired, and I am concerned about all the medications that he's on. I wonder if some of the meds were as much for the benefit of the staff taking care of him as for David.

He does still have some dramatic mood swings. He'll get really sad, really quick. It lasts a few minutes, and it's heartbreaking. You hug him and try to comfort him, and you hope that it helps. You just try to be there for him until it passes. And yes, he's on meds for this, too. I think he needs this one.

We're giving David a few days to adjust to being home before putting too much on him, therapy-wise. The therapist is coming by tomorrow (Wednesday) to do the initial evaluation and we've been looking at this as the kickoff for David's new therapy program.

Sunday, August 10, 2008
(McCleary)
David has been home with us for nine days, and I think he's
settling in pretty well. He's relaxed, comfortable, and is getting
used to things around here. He sleeps very soundly at night.

I also think he's communicating a little better. Occasionally
when he "talks" to me, he will choose his words in such a way
that I'm sure he's trying to make me understand rather than
just giving me the easy, standard responses.

He will also sometimes initiate communication in order to
change something in his surroundings, rather than just letting
things go the way they are. For instance, when waking from a
nap, he has asked us to turn on his television. We usually have
to ask him about such things.

Whenever I lay David down I always tell him to call out if he
needs anything and that I'll hear him (we have a monitor in his
room). In most cases, he never does. One afternoon, though,
he made sounds that suggested to me he wanted something.
When I went in, he looked up at me and stated "tea, please".
We usually have one cup with water and another with juice, ice
tea or Gatorade. We always have to anticipate and ask him if
he wants a drink, and will respond "fine" or "no".

He's still really big on the "fine" response, but I've been trying
to ask questions that need more than "fine" for an answer, and
when he tries to give it to me anyway, I'll reword my question.

Last night Ashley asked her dad a question that would normally
have brought out a "fine" response, and David instead said
"sure". I'm wondering if maybe he thought I would jump in if
he said "fine" and didn't want to have to deal with it.

David is still easily over-stimulated. More than a few minutes
with a handful of people in the room, and he may become very
agitated, angry, argumentative, and will start lashing out
verbally. On the other side of it, David and I have had a number
of opportunities this past week and a half to spend an
afternoon or even most of the day with just the two of us. He
seems very at peace then. We'll watch a movie or a tv show,
laugh at what we see, talk back and forth. It is during these

times that David will usually initiate a request or make a comment beyond the easy answers.

We keep David up for a few hours at a time, then take him into his room and let him rest for an hour or so. Sometimes he'll watch some television, usually after he's napped for twenty or thirty minutes.

David eats most of his meals in the dining room with us, though sometimes when it's just the two of us we'll eat in the living room with tv trays.

We've had the speech therapist, occupational therapist, physical therapist, and nurse all make visits to the house. They will each be making regular weekly or twice-weekly visits. David is going to be busy.

It was the speech therapist who after her evaluation session commented that David was definitely in there and we were going to bring him out.

Friday, August 15, 2008
(McCleary)
I believe David is showing real progress over the last week or so.

There have been a few speed bumps along the way, but in general David continues to get better, both physically and mentally.

On the mental side of things, David seems to be able to communicate ideas better, to put some sentences together, to concentrate better.

One thing that Sylvia and I were talking about just yesterday... when I would spend time with David in Palo Alto, more often than not it was very much a father and his five year old son. Now, since coming home, David and I have been able to spend a significant about of time together, just him and me. I no longer see the five year old boy looking up at his Dad. David is very much my adult son.

On the physical side of things, David is assisting more and more with all aspects of his care, as regards moving him, transferring him, dressing him. He has much more control of his arms and legs, responds very well when I ask him to help me with one thing or another.

He is now working well with his therapists, his occupational therapist in particular. The therapists are also able to work with David for longer periods of time.

His occupational therapist has made several very positive observations.

First of all, he has stated that he doesn't believe any of David's constrictions or other issues are permanent. He has stated that he thinks David will return close to 100%, although some of his problems will take some time.

He said that David's ankles/feet are at 90% and he's going to work to get that other 10%.

He doesn't want us to buy the hand pedal machine because he doesn't think David will need it for long. Instead he brought one to us that we can borrow.

Following the Occupational Therapist's second visit, he asked me what my own expectations were. I of course mentioned the Mt. Rainier climb in two years. The OT thought a moment, then said "With what I've seen with David, I think that's a perfectly reasonable goal".

For me, after getting so many of the sympathetic "you poor deluded father" looks whenever I brought up the idea of Mt. Rainier, having David's OT tell me that we can do this, I was ecstatic

Friday, August 22, 2008
(McCleary)
While I do believe that David is continuing to move ahead
cognitively, from a father's perspective it just seems so
painfully slow. Maybe I'm afraid that it'll all come to a stop and
it's all we'll get (here's your kid back, thanks a lot...)

I see the little things that tell me he's getting better; a word or
a phrase or a facial expression, and I'll think that he's back, and
then he'll have an episode (his mom will come in and place a
hand on his, tell him good night, and he'll suddenly fly into a
fit), and everything I saw throughout the day seems like an
illusion, and that I was deluding myself.

I'll tell myself to be patient, that he's better today than
yesterday. And that's true. He is better each day, both
physically and cognitively, but with both I have this horrible
feeling that there's a wall that David will not be able get past. I
just don't know where those walls are.

So we keep pushing. I've told other people often enough that
I'm not going to put any limits on where David will end up, and
I need to remember that. His progress has been advancing at a
tremendous rate since coming home when compared to his
time at the hospitals. When put up against the time since David
was first hurt, he's only been home a very short time.

But I want him back now. All the way.

Thursday, August 28, 2008
(McCleary)
David's O.T. (occupational therapist) has really been working to
find ways help David get better and keep him interested. He
was the one to have David stand up even though we don't have
a standing frame at the moment. He's been having me perform
different range-of-motion exercises with David in between O.T.
visits and has me working with David using the hand-pedal
machine.

On Tuesday, the O.T. eyed my recombinant bicycle and decided
that David could do that. He wheeled him over, transferred him
to the bicycle, had David hold on and told him to pedal. David

did fine, and he kept himself in a good sitting position. It's a nice recombinant bike, was recommended to me by my back doctor after I had recovered from my last surgery, but it isn't exactly designed for someone in David's situation. There's no strapping in. If he can stay in it and feel comfortable using it, that's great. He and I had the same back surgery, so if it's good for me, it should help strengthen his abdominal and back muscles, and it will certainly help with his lower-extremity range-of-motion and overall body strength.

I continue to see the little things cognitively that give us hope, things that would be easy for others to miss but not those of us who work with him constantly.

I had spent yesterday at work (I'm out of the house two days a week), so I hadn't seen David since the early morning. When I came home, I went in his room where he had been resting. Someone had turned his TV on. I sat beside him and waited for him to say something first. He glanced over at me, smiled at me, then looked back at the television. A few seconds later, he said "A good show". For me, that was a big wow moment.

Sometimes when he and I are watching television together, I'll ask him if he liked the show, or I'll say something like "that was pretty good, huh?", or "that was all right, kinda corny", or whatever. He'll agree and that's that. This time, he initiated it. Also, it wasn't a whispered comment. He spoke up in a normal (almost) tone of voice.

David still whispers his words most of the time, but he is speaking up more often. We know there's nothing physically wrong with his vocal chords (do we ever), so if we can't hear him we don't let it slide. We tell him we can't hear him and ask him to speak up. So now, at least occasionally, he speaks up on his own, without us having to ask him.

We continue to lessen his medications. At one time, we were giving him something like three dozen pills a day, half a dozen or more different kinds. We're gradually giving him fewer of each and have dropped some altogether (RN guidance). I think this is helping his focus, his ability to interact with those around him, and is helping to keep him in this world and not some foggy otherworld. I still believe some of the meds were more for the hospital staff and not for David.

Tuesday, September 02, 2008
(McCleary)
We took David out to breakfast the other day. We chose the restaurant right here in town, so it was nearby and quiet. He did pretty good, but we did have to keep the outing brief.

As for feeding himself, we're still using just the fork, and we have to "stab" the food for him. After a few bites, we'll usually take over. We don't want to stress him during his meals.

David continues to come up with new words and even some brief, two or three word sentences. Every few days, we'll hear something new. This gives me hope.

Physically, the occupational therapist is as positive as ever. David is a long way from being able to stand (without a lot of support), and when I transfer him from bed to chair or back again, I'm not sensing any improvement (I encourage him to help me), but his range of motion is improving, and I can usually get him to perform physical activity, such as pulling and pushing with his arms and legs.

He usually understands what I'm trying to ask him to do, though he can easily become confused. I take it slow, and let him know that he's in charge. More than anything, I want him to feel that he's in control of the world around him. I can sense that he's at his best when he feels that he can say yes or no, is free to make decisions about what's going to happen, can offer some direction.

Some have said that it's like taking care of a child, but I disagree with that analogy. While I do have to care for him as with an infant in many ways, I don't interact with him that way at all. I see this as a partnership between two adults. David has his role and I have mine, and together we're doing everything we can to bring him back.

Thursday, September 04, 2008
(McCleary)
Imagine a thin, gossamer veil between where David is now and
where he's going to be when he comes out of this.

I think that's all there is. That's how close he is.

Over the last few days, we've witnessed little things that have
us nearly ecstatic. Just a word or a comment or a facial
expression. Almost insignificant. And the fact that we are falling
over ourselves over such little things tells you that the two
worlds (where he is and where is needs to go) are very far
apart.

But all that's left is for him to pull aside that veil and walk
through.

I think he's that close. He still gets confused. He still does and
says things that brings back to me the fact that he's not
completely with us. But I do really believe he's almost back.

Physically, he has miles to go (all the way up that mountain I
keep talking about).

Cognitively, though, I believe there's just one more step for him
to take. It's a really, really, really big step, but it's just one more
step.

And... once he's back mentally, I think the physical recovery will
come more easily. It will still be very difficult, but he will be
able to take a more active role.

Thursday, September 11, 2008
(McCleary)
I think that everyone who interacts with David is pleased at the
progress he's shown cognitively over the past five weeks. Since
coming home, we've seen some amazing changes in the way he
deals with the world around him and his communication with
us.

But that last step that he needs to take is a major one, and I am
frequently reminded that he's not fully back with us. A word, or

a response to a request and there is no doubt that he's not quite there. But the hopeful signs are all there, we see them almost daily.

Physically, we're seeing more progress in some areas than in others.

His hands are showing improvement. I work with them twice a day, and I'm seeing more flexibility and strength in the fingers (except the "trigger" fingers) and in one wrist. His left wrist is still awfully constricted. Self-feeding is still very awkward, but he does try. This is also an area where I see that David isn't yet completely back with us. He will often lift his fork to his mouth in an automated reflex, not yet having tried to put anything on the fork.

Range of motion on his arms is improving some. Again, I work with him twice daily. He still can't lift them above his head using his shoulders, but I can get him to touch the top of his head with his hands by bending his elbows. After I work his elbows for a few minutes, I can almost straighten them.

I still haven't seen any improvement in his ability to "assist" me when I transfer him from bed to wheelchair or back again. I encourage him to bear his own weight and stand during the transfer, and while I can sense that he's trying, I'm not feeling much here.

We really need to get a standing frame apparatus, and while we're told that they're working on it, we have yet to see one.

Our "caregiver" schedule hasn't worked out exactly as planned, due primarily to Sylvia's work schedule and Sem's efforts to push David through the VA and Active Duty systems and Sem and Sylvia's efforts to sell David's old house in Oklahoma and buy a new home here in the northwest.

So I'm caregiver five days a week, and on Tuesdays and Wednesdays Sem and Sylvia are sharing the duty. Sem comes by when she can, and some days she and I will load David into the van and take him up to Madigan or the VA hospital at American Lake for an appointment.

In the evenings, Sylvia and I are working together.

And the evenings are growing a bit longer these days...

We used to get David settled into bed around 8:00. Once in bed, he might want to watch another half hour or so of television, but nonetheless he was settled in for the night.

This would give me a little time in the evening to take care of other things.

No more.

David isn't ready for bed at 8:00. He wants to stay up, and he wants to stay up with us.

He also wants to get up earlier each morning. And he seems to need less rest time during the day.

I think this is due to several factors. He is sleeping very soundly during the night, and his brain is needing less "down time" to process his daily experiences. This is all to the good.

Final tidbit: The other day I was telling David about how he and I are both in training for the Mt. Rainier climb. He said "Good. Good." A few minutes later, we're watching the news and behind the news anchors is the image of Mt. Rainier. I point this out to David. "There's the mountain, David." I could swear the look he gave me was something along the lines of "Are you crazy?"

Monday, September 22, 2008
(McCleary)
Sem got the house that she and Sylvia have been working on. She and the kids are moving in this week. There is going to be some work done on it to make it more handicap accessible, but she would still like to have David there with her now, so we're going to be moving him as well.

As I mentioned in the last update, we're all glad to see the continuing progress during his time with us, coming up on a couple of months now, though of course we would like to see more.

David shows continuing improvement in self-feeding. Our meals together take longer, but he's doing better at using both a fork and a spoon. He's as patient with me as I am with him. Things can get messy, but you can see that he's proud of his accomplishment.

For a snack, I will sometimes set a can of cashews in his lap. It took a few weeks, but he can now put his hand into the can and pull out cashews. He ends up with more than few on his chest and belly, but more make it into his mouth every day.

And we had another improvement on that front just yesterday. David looked down and saw a cashew sitting on his chest that had fallen. He reached down, picked it up and put it into his mouth. Thought processing-wise, I think that was significant.

I perform range-of-motion exercises with him twice a day, shoulders, elbows, wrists and fingers, knees and ankles. Greater flexibility is showing improvement in all his other efforts, and he and I work together as a team in all these things. He's even started to help me more during our morning session where we get cleaned up and ready for the day.

And... three days in a row he's shown that he wants to work on bathroom training. He and I have been working on this one in private and so this is all I'll be saying about this.

David and I have become really close. We've been inseparable during his two months here and I'm going to miss him a lot.

He and I have our routine. First, each morning rise and shine, clean up, get dressed, have breakfast, and wait on the therapist. After his morning therapy session, we usually watch a little TV together before lunch. Lunch is a therapy session in itself, but he's getting better and better. Afterward, we usually have another therapist drop by, and we work another couple of hours. We usually have to clean up a bit then, and then maybe he'll lay down for half an hour or so. Later in the afternoon, we'll do range of motion exercises and talk about our plans. Sylvia comes home and we talk about our day. We have dinner, then relax and watch television for a couple of hours. We "talk" together a lot about what we're watching. He has shows that he likes, and shows he doesn't (He likes Stargate Atlantis, Burn Notice, reruns of Scrubs, Red Dwarf and Star Trek Enterprise). At some point during our TV time, we'll have a snack in the living room in front of the television, usually some fruit. Later in the evening we'll go to his room and get him settled in for the night. It takes us about half an hour. Once he's settled in, we'll turn on his television and he'll spend some alone time. We'll usually turn the TV off about 11:00. It's a long but rewarding day. Next morning, we do it again.

He and I have been talking about his upcoming move to his new house and with his wife and kids. We talk about how he's going to get to go back to being a family, being a Dad, he and Sem together again. I think he's excited about it, but I can also sense anxiety. It's bound to be a scary time. The change is going to be scary, and leaving the safety and security that we've created for him here has to be scary.

I would have liked for David to take that "last step" and be fully back with us cognitively before leaving, but I can certainly understand Sem wanting him with her. And... his house is only five minutes from my office, so I'll be dropping in on them and making a nuisance of myself on a regular basis.

Olympia

Sunday, September 28, 2008

Well, we moved David over to his new house and he seems to be doing okay.

He was anxious beforehand, and after Sylvia and I left him with his family the first day he became nauseous, but after a restless first night he settled down and is enjoying being with his wife and kids.

I had been working with David on using the WII game console (sports games) before the move, and his family has been keeping that going. You need to help him of course, but he's getting better and it's great at increasing flexibility and dexterity, mental processing, and coordination.

He loves to get out on the road, and Sem takes him in their van when she runs errands.

She hasn't scheduled the therapists to start coming to their house yet, but I'm hoping that'll start soon. I don't want David to backslide on his therapies. They don't have any equipment there yet, but that should be coming soon and the therapists can do a lot in the meantime.

The modifications haven't started on the house as yet, either. I built a ramp to make it easier to get David into and out of the house, but there is a lot of work that needs to be done; widening the hallway and doors, modifying the shower, permanent ramps.

Since their house is only a few minutes from the office, I'll be going to see David once or twice a week during my lunch breaks, and Sylvia and I will be going over there on weekends. I'm also hoping Sem will bring him over to our house now and then. We can visit and play games, and hey, our house is already handicap adapted...

Monday, October 06, 2008
We had a family dinner in a restaurant this weekend to celebrate my birthday; Sylvia and me, David and his family, Christy and her family.

David seemed happy, and did pretty well despite the noise in the small room that we had reserved and the sounds coming in from the main floor of the restaurant (The room was open to the rest of the place).

He smiled a number of times, was very observant of what everyone was doing, would smile or chuckle when someone did or said something funny. He also did a pretty good job of feeding himself.

He had told Sem what he wanted his family to get me for my birthday. They gave me season one of Stargate: Atlantis on DVD. He and I had watched a lot of that show when he was staying with us, and now that he is with his family, Sem has been buying the series for him.

David and Sem had gone shopping in the morning, and so I asked him where he went. He will usually say "I don't know". This time he said "Fred Meyer", and it was perfectly understandable.

He's been in his new house for a couple of weeks now, and the therapy team still isn't visiting him. They need to get this going again. I'm starting to get concerned, as I don't want any backsliding.

I don't see any backsliding cognitively. I'm seeing him two or three times a week now that he's with his family, and there is at least some sign of progress with every visit. This last time it was "Fred Meyer" instead of "I don't know". Little things like that are really, really big.

Tuesday, October 14, 2008
David's therapists have started back up, so David once again has company (other than family) dropping by on a regular schedule. We still don't have the larger pieces of equipment for him, but I'm glad to see therapy back in the picture. We need to get him rolling over, sitting up, standing, and walking. The first two he does only with assistance, and the second two need to happen so that David and I can start training for our little climbing adventure scheduled for the Summer of 2010.

David likes to be involved in the conversations going on around him, and will listen intently to everything being said. He won't speak in full sentences, but he does interject a word now and then into the discussion, and the occasional two word phrases.

The other day I was sitting next to him while I was working with Kevin on state capitals. Kevin and Ashley mentioned a trip that their Dad had taken them on to "someplace in Mississippi". The kids were looking in an atlas when one of them said that they had gone to "Natchez", a town in Mississippi.

David had been listening and spoke up, saying "Indian name", and I believe he said "tribe".

The Natchez Tribe is right outside Natchez, Mississippi. I'm guessing that on that trip they took, David learned a bit of the history of the area. Speaking up the way he did would indicate that the memories of the trip and of what he had learned on that trip came flooding back during our conversation.

I'm waiting for the day when we can all sit around the table and have a conversation wherein David is speaking in full sentences. It's more than just having him string a series of words together into a meaningful phrase, though of course that will be huge. But from a personal side, I need to be able to hear his voice again. Pushing out one and two words at a time allows David to get the meaning across, but it doesn't give us a chance to really hear his voice.

And even when he does string more than two words together, he pushes them out so fast that it's not very clear and it's not his voice.

I remember the first time we heard him breathe without the trach in his throat. We commented excitedly that we actually "heard" him for the first time since the incident.

I remember when David first started pushing out those single words, and the first time we understood what he was saying. We knew that some of David was in there. And he was speaking to us. And it was his voice... or so we thought at the time.

Sylvia ran across the "memory dial" on her phone for Little David's cell phone. She pressed it and got David's voice mail. That's David's voice. Sylvia got very emotional. It really hit home that we have yet to hear our boy's voice.

We need to hear that voice.

After all, when he and I are standing on top of Mt. Rainier, I plan on he and I having a conversation about what we've just accomplished and the scene spread out before us.

Monday, October 20, 2008
David and his family came over to our house for a visit on Saturday. My brother Jerry and his wife Lisa were here and we all spent a few hours sitting around talking. David was in a great mood. He didn't say very much, but he nonetheless appeared to be very involved in all that was going on and he enjoyed himself.

Jerry and Lisa had their grandson with them, and David was all smiles watching everything the kid did.

On Sunday Sylvia and I went over to David's house so that Sem could get away for a while to do some shopping on her own. She often takes David with her (and he enjoys it), but getting away by herself now and then is important.

While she was gone, David and I watched some football and we all just sat around talking. He was in another good mood.

There is one really important observation to mention. While he did speak up with more of those one word comments of his (for instance, when Kevin asked what the Cincinnati team was, his dad said "Bengals", and David told Ashley that the car he had when he was a teenager was "automatic"), David also managed to string several words together into short sentences, and he spoke up clearly enough that I understood some of them. When David's dog stood up and barked in the direction of the front door, David turned to Ashley and said "Your Mom's home." He didn't say just "mom" or "Sem". That's good stuff.

And speaking of David's dogs, David will hold his hand out and say "Come here" to them. When they come, he says "sit", and once they're sitting he'll pat them on the head. More good stuff.

All in all, I would say that progress continues.

Friday, October 24, 2008
It was on this date last year (October 24, 2007) that David opened his eyes for the first time since closing them October 12th, 2007.

He was still in the lowest levels of consciousness, and it would be a week before we saw the first hints of tracking movement, and much longer before anyone believed us when we said that we saw his eyes track.

But opening his eyes that first time was first step in getting from there to here. We still have such a long way to go, but we have come a very long way.

It has indeed been a journey.

Tuesday, November 04, 2008

David hasn't been improving much physically lately, and is actually backsliding some. I'm afraid that everyone may be getting just a little too comfortable with the way things are and may be letting other issues get in the way of pushing David. Still, the therapists are coming and working with him, and I am hopeful that he will begin making strides forward again soon.

Cognitively, there are no great strides forward, but David does continue to make his wants known. By this I mean that he hasn't progressed any further toward speaking in a normal conversational way, but he is initiating interaction more and doesn't just wait for you to ask a question.

The other day he suddenly told his physical therapist "You're done." He then turned to Sem and said "Shopping." When Sem asked "shopping for what", he said "presents". Turned out he wanted presents for himself, although when I asked about the remote control car they bought, David smiled and said "Kevin". I don't think so.

Another day, David looked at Sem and said "I'm ready." When she asked "ready for what?", he said "Denny's". She thinks that he saw a commercial earlier in the day, because Denny's isn't high on his list of places to go.

David does like to get out of the house. This is one sign of progress that I am particularly happy to see. Getting out in public and having to deal with a number of external stimuli going on at once helps David better deal with noisy family gatherings, something we are still working on. He does still get over stimulated, but is improving.

So, all in all, he continues to get better each week, though you do sometimes really have to look for it. But you take what you can get and do what you can to see that the progress doesn't stop.

Monday, November 10, 2008

The other day David said that he wanted his teeth fixed. I don't know the exact words he used, but Sem said that she didn't prompt him, he just said it. I know that in the past I've talked with David about it, and the subject has come up during conversation while he was present, but I still think that David bringing it up on his own is important, and for several reasons.

First of all, David was thinking about the fact that he was missing his teeth and felt it important enough to state that he wanted them fixed, for whatever reason. I know that he can have difficulty eating with his two front teeth missing. He may have been mentally processing his mealtime problem and reasoned that if he had his teeth, it would be less complicated.

Secondly, I have been urging David to speak out on his own when he wants something. He does so occasionally, but for the most part he'll wait to be asked or prompted. Stating flatly that he wants his teeth fixed is very, very different than responding to the question "do you want your teeth fixed"?

Sylvia has spent the last few days telling everyone that "David had another spark". I think she may be right. It is certainly encouraging.

A few other items of note...

Sylvia and I spent the other evening with David when Sem had to take Kevin up to the hospital (he broke his hand last Friday). Not so good for Kevin, but we nonetheless had a nice evening with David. Ashley stayed with us and did a good job as hostess. She made us hamburgers, and we watched a movie and talked.

The next day we met them all at Red Lobster for lunch. I asked for a quiet area and they found a great spot for us. David handled it very well, and there was just enough distraction to keep him aware that he was out in public. We don't want to protect him too much. Every such activity is a therapy session, though I try to make a big deal about it.

I do think that David is speaking in sentences a bit more. Sometimes I believe he will use a single word just because it's easier than having to string together a set of words, especially as we often can't understand what he's saying, which only frustrates him. I sense that he is thinking in complete sentences and then giving us the one word translation.

I don't want to read too much into it yet. Our conversations are still a bit stilted, but I am often pleased at what I hear. I will ask a question as casually and calmly as I can and he will often give me an equally casual reply that my healthy, grown son would be expected to come up with. Unfortunately, as I've said before, minutes later he will then do or say something that makes it all too clear that he's not completely back. I think these moments are becoming less frequent, but they are still with us. And, there are other areas in David's cognitive recovery that are still progressing very slowly, if at all.

But, the sparks that Sylvia talks about are still happening. We're not done yet and this has been a pretty good week.

Monday, November 17, 2008
David went to the movies the other day. He handled it very well. Afterward, he called to tell me (Sem called and put him on speaker). Sem had to prompt him a bit about where they had gone (first he said 'shopping', then he said 'mall' when Sem started the word with 'm', but then he did finally say "movies". I asked him what he had gone to see, and he said 'Madagascar'. He said it fairly clearly.

This is good news for several reasons.

First of all, he was able to handle a matinee showing of Madagascar. I don't think I could have handled that.

Second, David still likes to say "I don't know" when you ask him a question. He didn't do that this time, and it was a follow-up question. He named the movie that he saw.

Finally, I understood him when he said the name of the movie. To be honest, Ashley had already told me that they had gone to see Madagascar, but I really think that he said it clearly enough that I would have understood him anyway. Sure, it was his fast mumble, but it was understandable nonetheless.

We went up to American Lake and David sat through a series of Botox shots. He was very brave about it, but he sure knows how to give a good glare.

The shots were given in several locations in the muscles of both forearms and it's hoped they will help loosen up his wrists and fingers, and perhaps prevent the need for surgery to cut the tendons.

Ron, his occupational therapist, was ecstatic when I told him that David had finally gotten a new series of Botox injections and will be focusing all the more on David's hands. He thinks there is going to be real progress over the next few weeks.

Ron also told me the other day that he would like very much to be a part of our climb up Mt. Rainier. He first said that he was going to be contacting someone he knew with both climbing and therapy experience, but then said that he would like to be part of the team himself, doesn't want to turn David over to someone else after spending so much time with him. I said that would be great, let's just make sure David's ready to begin training next May. He said we should start with some one day excursions in the lower elevations...

Sure sounds to me like I've found someone as confident as I am about David, and someone more objective and who would know...

And I think Sem might be starting to think it could just happen... After I told her about what Ron said, she later had a little talk with David. She said "So as soon as we get you all better, your Dad's going to take you up a mountain so you can get hurt again. I'm going to kick his butt." David said "No you're not." She asked "I'm not going to kick his butt?" David answered "No. You're not."

When she told me about this, she said that my son was protecting me...

Sunday, November 30, 2008

David and his family came over for Thanksgiving, and I think he enjoyed himself, though by the time they left it was clear that he was ready to head home. He was getting a little agitated. There was a lot going on.

Sylvia laid out a major Thanksgiving dinner and we opened the table out to its full length to accommodate the three families. David didn't eat a lot, but was very attentive to the conversations around the table. Afterward, we sat around the living room and talked about when David and his sister were kids. David remembered each of the often told stories, and laughed at most of them.

The next day we took David to the dentist to begin the process to have implants put in. If you remember, his two front teeth had to be taken out when we were at Walter Reed.

He handled this first step pretty well. He had to have a number of X-rays taken, his teeth had to be thoroughly examined by the dentist, and finally he had to have a mold impression made. This involved keeping the mouthpiece with the mold material in his mouth for a full three minutes. To be honest, we didn't think he would sit still for this, but he did great.

This cast will be sent up to a facility in Seattle, David's next stop. Having implants put in is a long, multi-stage process, but one that David is eager to do. He really wants his teeth.

Yesterday Sylvia and I went to Cabela's Outfitters to do a recon to see if it would be something that David would like. Yes, it is just a sporting goods store done up to look like a 'destination location', but it is kinda cool, especially if you're into any of the activities that they outfit. Sylvia and I spent a couple of hours sightseeing in there. That's saying something; I hate shopping, so you better give me more than walking up and down the aisles and saying 'oh, isn't this just adorable'...

We think David might like to visit Cabela's, providing we go early enough to avoid crowds. After we look at some of the exhibits, we can check out their boating department, fishing department, and I may have a look at their hiking boots and backpacks.

Sunday, December 21, 2008
David is supposed to be traveling up to Seattle next week for his first preparatory visit to the dentist that will be doing the implant surgery. With the weather what it is, I don't know whether he's going to make that appointment. His initial visit a few weeks ago was to a dentist at American Lake, but now he has to go further north for a series of visits that will span several months.

Speaking of weather, we're getting word that David has a bit of cabin fever. He doesn't like being trapped at home, wants to get out and about. He enjoyed the snow at first, but now it's just keeping him shut in, and he's not happy about that.

Cognitively, I think David is a bit sharper over these past few weeks, and some of this may be due to Sem continuing to back him off his meds. However, I don't believe we're where we should be. Yes, you can ask him a question and he will respond. Sometimes his response is quite clear, other times you can figure out what he is trying to say. He's also speaking more sentences, although here he is less clear. And we are a long way from having what can be considered a normal conversation. Perhaps as we get further from the medications that he was on for so long, we'll begin to see more significant improvement. At least, I'm hoping it will help.

As for his physical status, I am growing increasingly concerned. I'm not seeing much improvement. For a number of reasons, David isn't getting the consistent therapy that he needs. He really needs therapy sessions every day, and he's not getting them. Not even close. Additionally, we still don't have the equipment that he needs.

I'm also beginning to feel like we're falling into a pattern of "make David comfortable" more than "make David better". I am afraid that if he doesn't get back to a pattern of a daily routine of pushing himself both physically and cognitively that the David we have now is the David that we're going to have for the rest of his life. We all see clear signs from David that he wants to get better, that he "sees" where he is and wants to move forward (in particular, he wants to walk), and we need to keep that fire going.

On a completely different note... David has a ceremony coming up, probably sometime in February. He will be receiving his Bronze Star, his Purple Heart, and will be given his discharge in a presentation ceremony. I know that some of you have indicated an interest in attending, so I'll let you know as date and time are more certain.

Saturday, January 03, 2009
David made the first trip to Seattle to see the VA dentist that will be doing the implant surgery. They did some more prep work. They'll be putting him under when they do the surgery, which is still a little ways off.

With the improvement in road conditions, David and his family have been making trips to the movies. Sylvia and I joined them to see The Day the Earth Stood Still at an IMAX screen. It was the first IMAX experience for Sylvia and me. Pretty cool. David didn't seem as impressed, but then so far as movies go, he's more into Adam Sandler than science fiction. Sem says he laughed through most of a comedy they had gone to a couple of days before.

David knows his actors, though. When we were gathered in the lobby after the movie, Ashley was talking about the main star. Without prompting, her father clearly said "Keanu Reeves", and he said it correctly. Most people, if they know the name at all, usually get the pronunciation wrong.

We celebrated David's birthday last weekend. We all went to one of those Japanese restaurants where they prepare your food in front you, and where the chef flings bits of food at you and you're supposed to try to catch it in your mouth. We had a pretty good time, but by the end of the day David had had 'happy birthday' sung to him about five times. When it was all done, he was ready to call it a day.

His standing frame is supposed to be arriving soon... finally. After all this time, I hope the anticipation isn't greater than the reality. But we've all seen what David can do, and to have been deprived of the equipment all this time has prevented any possibility of progress. If he's going to get back on his feet, this is necessary. If you haven't yet seen the "first steps" video, have a look. It shows what he was able to accomplish months ago with a simple walker and a couple of determined therapists. We haven't seen him up like that since. I'm really looking forward to the next few months. Maybe 2009 will be the year it all comes together.

Monday, January 26, 2009
From my perspective at least, David seemed to be stuck in a rut these past few weeks. I saw very few signs of improvement either physically or mentally.

Over the last couple of visits with him, though, we have seen some indicators that he might be ready for another push forward, at least cognitively. He's coming up with new responses to questions and situations, choosing to bypass some of the easy, overly-used responses we've been hearing these past months. Also, while in the past I've frequently heard humor that I would expect more from someone much younger, I've begun to hear more of David's true sense of humor. Sem is telling us of similar interactions and of more conversational exchanges he is having with her and with the kids.

There does seem to be more of the real David showing through the last week or so. I'm encouraged by this.

There is something that I am worried about, though. David has begun to stutter. I don't know if it's because he is ever more aware and is trying harder, or if there's something new physically that is showing itself and that we need to be concerned about. We need to look into it further and talk with his therapists.

Still no standing frame! David is so ready to get out of his chair and still we have no equipment. If I had known that it would take this long, we would have bought the thing ourselves months ago. We keep expecting it any time, and so we wait rather than go out and buy one on our own. That, and then a walker (much, much less expensive...).

No set date yet on the ceremony for his Bronze Star and Purple Heart. It may get pushed to March, but I don't yet know for sure.

Friday, February 06, 2009
Well, a couple of things happened over the last week or so...

We all got together and watched the Super Bowl. I think David enjoyed the day. We sat around and ate junk, drank near-beer, and talked about everything, occasionally the game. It was a pretty good game.

And... we finally have the standing frame! Hydraulics get him up and a lot of gear keeps him up, and he seems to be doing very well with it. Sem will get him into it and keep him on his feet for an hour at a time. It's great to see him on his feet again, even if he's all strapped in to keep him that way. It's a great step, and considering how well he does, it's only a first step to good things ahead.

We finally have word on David's ceremony. He will be receiving his Bronze Star and his Purple Heart on February 23rd at 1:00 at Fort Lewis. I guess they want to give him his medals before his discharge, which is set for the end of the month.

The ceremony was to be held in an auditorium, but there was concern that a large venue and an event open to the general public (and a lot of soldiers doing the 'hoo-rah') might be overwhelming for David. So it's going be held in a smaller building. We're supposed to meet at the gate, where they will have vans waiting to take us in.

Thursday, February 19, 2009
David's ceremony is still on for next Monday, Feb 23rd, at 1:00. If you're coming and you haven't yet told Sylvia or me, you need to contact one of us so that we can get your name on the list to get you cleared through post security ahead of time. We're meeting at the visitor's center at the main gate before the ceremony, where they'll be loading us into vans to take us in.

David seems to be very excited about this, mostly because a few days later he will be officially retiring out.

He is using his standing frame regularly, though I don't know how often. Sem says that he's able to stand for long stretches at a session. I'm hoping this is but a short step to using a walker, and then a cane, and then just walking. Remember that video of him being assisted using a walker all those months ago? There's no reason we shouldn't be far beyond that stage by now.

In my mind's eye, I see David rolling over and sitting up on his own, being helped into his walker, and then guided to the bathroom, to his exercise bike, to the dining table, to wherever.

None of that is happening now, but I'm hoping it comes soon. I want so much for David to be able to start doing things with Sem and the kids. And then of course there's that little activity that his mom and I have started training for.

Yes, I'm trying to draw her into the climb. To be able to stand on the summit with her son, after all that has happened... I just don't want her to miss that.

Tuesday, February 24, 2009
David's award ceremony was held on Monday, February 23, at
12:30 PM, the Warrior Transition Brigade at Fort Lewis, where
he was presented the Bronze Star and the Purple Heart.

There was about a dozen or so family there, and even more
soldiers.

David looked very happy and very proud, decked out in his
Class A's. It took some doing getting him into it, Sylvia and Sem
and I had to work at it a while, but he was patient with us. The
constriction of his arms gave us trouble. Also, we kept popping
off the clips that hold all his medals and ribbons to his uniform.

During the presentation, the commander mentioned
something that I hadn't known. David was on his 150th combat
mission when he was injured. When I went up to his sergeant
later and asked "150??", he nodded and said "you ought to see
his file. It goes on forever", and then he said that David is the
most highly decorated soldier to go through there (the Warrior
Transition Brigade).

I'm guessing (don't know for sure) that some of the 150 combat
missions were those he went on during his tour in Bosnia /
Kosovo. I can't imagine all 150 in the nine months he was in
Afghanistan, especially since many lasted weeks.

Several of David's Afghanistan missions were located in the
Khyber Pass at the Afghanistan / Pakistan border. Again, I'm
not sure, but I think his Bronze Star came from one of these
and the Purple Heart several weeks later from another.

As the commander spoke, I could see David going through
different emotions. He beamed proudly when the commander
talked of David training the Afghanis to stand on their own, of
how David was a soldier that other soldier's looked to. David's
eyes reddened and teared up several times. I think that was the
case for a lot of us.

They let me pin the medals on him. I had wanted to from the
moment the subject of an award ceremony came up, but I
didn't say anything. But I jumped at it when the commander
asked me.

Afterward, everyone lined up to shake David's hand. I think he
sat straighter and prouder when it came time for the soldiers to
take their turn.

A photographer took a lot of pictures, during the ceremony and
group photos afterward. When I get my hands on them, I'll put
some on the website.

Once all the different "family group" pictures were done, the
commander asked David if he would like to take one with the
troops. David gave a very emphatic yes, so all in uniform were
called up front and gathered round.

I think David needed the acknowledgement of his service and
sacrifice from fellow soldiers. He needed to have them say to
him that he had done good.

One more thing I'd like to mention... David would really like to
see more of his sister. When we went over to his house before
the ceremony to help Sem get him ready, Sylvia said to him
"we brought Christy with us". David quickly lifted up his head
and asked "where is she?" and smiled when he saw her. We all
saw the look on his face. And later during the group photos,
there was one with just the two of them. The way he was
smiling at her as she came up to kneel beside him... he does
miss her. They were very close growing up, and I'm sure he has
emotions and feelings wrapped up in those childhood
memories. She doesn't get a chance to see him nearly enough.

Wednesday, March 11, 2009
First a warning... I'm frustrated.

Things have been too quiet lately, which is my way of saying
that David isn't progressing much at all. It's not his fault. His
therapy sessions aren't consistent and aren't frequent enough.
He has three different types of therapy: occupational, physical
and speech. If each therapist was to see him twice a week, then
he should be having at least (let's do the math here) six
sessions each and every week. I don't think he's getting a third
of that, and he can go weeks without one type of therapy or

another. So rather than moving forward, I think he's sliding back in many areas.

This makes me very much "not happy". Angry, actually. This doesn't have to be. I've seen the progress that he can make. I know what he's capable of. This isn't blind, wide-eyed, ever-hopeful, blubbering father emotion here. There needs to be some focus and some attention going on that isn't.

Okay, enough ranting... I should direct this where it will do some good.

And so, on a completely different note...

David is going to be coming over to stay with his mom and me at least once a month for a weekend visit. This will get him out of the house for more than just a shopping trip or a visit to the doctor, and it will give Sem a break for longer than just an afternoon. He has indicated that he wants to come over and we think it's a good idea.

I try to see him during the week at lunch as I can, and Sylvia and I go over on the weekends, but having him here at the house over a weekend will be nice.

Wednesday, March 18, 2009
We've seen some signs over the last week or two that David's brain is quietly going about its rewiring, however slowly that progress might be.

He's quicker to tell you his observations ("squirrel... climbing tree"). He really likes the squirrels living in his back yard. He's kind of fond of the crows, too.

He used to give you mostly one word responses, though not always. Now, if you ask him a question he's just as likely to give you a full sentence answer. It's often difficult to know what he said, but he's quite insistent about it. And he'll show his frustration when you don't understand.

He also seems to finally be ready for some of his other (more private) training. Sylvia and I cried over this one. We really,

really want to see progress here. It will be life-altering for David and for his family.

As for his therapy sessions... well... nothing new since the last status update rant, so I'll not go there.

Wednesday, March 25, 2009
We've been having some issues with VA since David's status changed from active duty to veteran.

The VA has been standing with David going all the way back to Walter Reed. They met with us during those first days to make sure everything would run smooth. Later, we met with representatives a number of times in Palo Alto. They became so involved with us while we were at Puyallup that the military had to ask them to ease up. They came out to my house and met with us for several hours. Papers were prepared, reviewed, and signed.

But as soon as David was discharged, it was as if VA didn't even know him. Everything is back to square one. Financial, medical, physical, everything. They're holding up his pay until a "competency determination" has been made. Well, that was already done and documented. And now they are even holding up his therapy. It's all at a standstill. Sigh... maybe I need to call Patty Murray.

Meanwhile, Sem bought a tabletop pedal machine (for both hands and feet). With the combination of the Botox injections of a few weeks ago and his daily work at the machine, we're seeing some real improvement with David's wrists and shoulders. He's much more limber. He can straighten his wrists (even bend one wrist back) and he can hold his arms up above his head (not quite straight, but definitely over his head).

I'd like to see more control and strengthening of his leg muscles. He has an exercise bicycle, but if this smaller machine is more convenient, maybe it will be used more frequently. If he can control the movement in his legs, then with the strength that he is already building in his legs, he can start using a walker.

If there was a way I could fast-track therapist certification so that I could get paid to work with him myself, I'd become his therapist and we could work together every day. Certification or not, there's just no way that I could afford to take the time away from a paying position to take over his sessions, even going part time. So we need to rely on outside therapists to come in regularly (but they're not) and for Sem to do what she can.

David is talking more and more, though much of it is very difficult to understand. He will also throw out words or sentences that, while you can understand them, may not be quite right. For instance, we were talking about the cost of physical therapy training and I said that one school was much more expensive than another. David piped up with "twenty dollars". He had the subject right (money), but was a bit off as to the value. I told him that it cost a little more than that. So he said "twenty one dollars". Hmm. Twenty one is more than twenty. He was incrementing. From that perspective, very good. But at that moment at least, he didn't have a realistic picture of what something might cost.

As for David's other um, more private training, there hasn't been much progress there.

Still, cognitively, taking the good with the not-so-good, it really does appear that his brain is working hard to rewire and reroute, as I mentioned in the last update. There are more sparks, there are more synapses firing, there's more connection going on.

But geez, it is so agonizingly slow, and the setbacks are so heartbreaking.

Overall, he's better this month than last month... and last month was better than the month before...

Twenty one is more than twenty...

David will be coming over Friday afternoon and staying with us until Monday. Looking forward to it.

Tuesday, March 31, 2009
David spent Friday thru Monday with us. It was a very rewarding weekend, and we all really enjoyed the time together.

During his time with us, David talked constantly. He was happy and very communicative. One thing I should note, though... it was like talking with Ozzy Osborne. A lot of conversation, with a lot of the words mumbled and grumbled together. The words are all there, and it all means something, but you need to decipher it. The more time we spent with him, the easier it got. I have ringing and buzzing in my ears, which doesn't help.

When we watched television, he pointed out everything that caught his attention. I also found that it was best to let the commercials run, because he knows them all by heart and likes to speak all the lines as they are being spoken by the actors. He's very good and has a sharp memory for these things. It is also much easier to understand what David is saying, partly because I can match his words to the commercial, but also because David speaks more clearly when reciting commercials. He's better with tempo and inflection. I'm guessing that this would be good for David, and this is saying something, as I am not one to readily apply value to any commercial. I generally avoid them at all cost.

We also watched a Spring training baseball game, a soccer game, and a couple of movies. He was very attentive to the Mariners game, but I think that of all we watched, he liked the cornball "Caveman" movie the best. He and I talked about it for hours afterward. I would bring up a scene, and as soon as he knew what scene I was going to mention, he would start laughing.

David has strong opinions about Afghanistan. When the subject comes up on the news, he listens carefully to what is being said and then speaks up, lets them and us know whether or not he agrees with what he's heard.

Sylvia, David and I had all our meals at the kitchen table, which sits in front of a window that overlooks our front yard. The yard is landscaped to be very bird friendly, and this time of year there's a lot of activity. David loved it. Once when we were sitting at the table and were talking about a baby hummingbird, David said, without prompting, "I like the window." When I looked at him, he said "I enjoy it." Strange, I don't think I've ever heard him say the word "enjoy" before...

We have a Bowflex set up in the exercise room, and it's configured so that we can roll David's wheelchair into position. We used it every day, and David had a blast. It works well for range of motion, increased flexibility, strengthening and conditioning. It was a lot of fun.

Sem called each night. As soon as the phone would ring, David would look expectantly at his mom (I seldom answer the phone). As soon as he knew it was Sem calling, he would get a big grin. His face would light up when Sylvia put the phone to his ear and he heard Sem's voice.

Christy brought Kim and Megan over for a few hours, and we all played Yahtzee in the library. There's a good sized table in there, and David was able to watch everyone and follow all the conversations. He really likes listening to his nieces.

Each time it was David's turn, I would put the cup in his hand and he would turn it over and dump the dice out. I could occasionally get him to shake the cup once or twice, but it was mostly dump and then see what the dice showed.

I would suggest an option and he would answer "okay" or "yes I think so"
or something similar.

David's sister won, but he came in second. After the game I asked him if he liked playing Yahtzee. He answered "Yes, very much. I liked it a lot."

I think that David is going out of his way not to answer questions with just one word, or even with one sentence. It seems as though he wants to give us multi-sentence answers.

He was all smiles when Sem came to pick him up Monday morning. He had missed her. She was an hour later than we expected, so there were frequent glances to the window between ten and eleven that morning. When the van pulled up he said that she was here. He told her that he had "been waiting for a long time".

Once loaded up in the van, David smiled and waved goodbye. When I had asked him earlier about coming again next month, he had said "Yes I want to. I am looking forward to it".

But like any vacation, no matter how much fun you have, it's always good to go home.

Tuesday, April 07, 2009
Sylvia and I met David and Sem at the VA Medical Facility up at American Lake this past Monday morning.

He needed to visit a number of different doctors up there, so Sem set the appointments up to all be on the same day so that we could get them all done at once. His first was at 10 AM, and we got out of the last one about 5:00.

It was a long day, but David handled it very well. We had a couple of breaks, including lunch at the canteen. In early afternoon we had half an hour or so to sit in the sun in a small park. We had ice cream and talked. A lady came by with a small dog on a leash. The dog introduced herself to each of us, and jumped up and put her front paws on David to that he could pet her. This of course had David smiling and chuckling.

David sure has something about dogs. Remember down in Palo Alto when the recreational therapist brought a dog in to see David? That was the first time we saw him smile.

Overall, David seemed to be okay most of the day. There was enough variety, and we had time between some of the appointments to just sit and visit.

His last appointment was at 4:00 PM, and by that time we could tell that David was about finished. He was patient, but the humor really wasn't there anymore (how would your humor hold up after a day of appointments at VA?). Still, he didn't show his frustration the way he would have in the past. I'll take that as progress.

For those who missed last week's update, be sure to go to the "previous updates" page and check it out. David spent a few days with us and it was a rewarding experience.

Wednesday, April 15, 2009
I was witness to something pretty amazing yesterday (Tuesday).

David is going to be spending more time at our house over the next few weeks while their house is being remodeled to accommodate his needs.

I am, of course, hoping that many of those needs are temporary, and yesterday I saw something to keep those hopes alive.

His physical therapist came over in the morning and spent several hours with him. About midway through the session came a certain exercise...

With the therapist supporting David on the left, and Sem supporting him on the right, leaving me to hold the wheelchair, David was helped to his feet (much of the work his own). The therapist then tapped the back of David's left leg and David moved it forward. The therapist then tapped the back of his right leg and David moved that leg forward.

In this way, David walked across the room. Yes, he was supported under both arms, but David did the work to move his legs and take the steps, and both of those supporting him said that David was carrying much of his own weight.

I followed along behind with the wheelchair, and after David had taken eight or ten steps, they set him back down.

We then changed position so that David would have a longer way to go. He didn't do quite as good this second time, but it wasn't that he wasn't trying. You can see that he really wants to do this.

The therapist is talking about getting a special walker for David to start working with. Oh, yeah...

Tuesday, April 21, 2009
"I'm not stupid, I'm wounded."

Jill Bolte Taylor said this in her book "My Stroke of Insight", in which she recounted her own journey. Jill Taylor is a brain scientist who in 1996 suffered a rare form of stroke. She could not walk, talk, read, write or recall any of her life. She spent eight years recovering. From the very morning of her stroke, Jill managed to "observe" what was happening to her. Even when she had no language and found herself separate from the world and her own past, even to the point of losing what we might think of as "self" and becoming "one with the universe", she was there.

While there are a number of differences between Jill's experience and David's, the similarities are unsettling. I see this more and more as David continues to recover.

A couple of things that really jumped out at me when reading the book:

It was important to Jill that those she came in contact with should treat her as though she was going to completely recover. David continues to improve week after week, but his real progress occurs when we target making him better, not with simply making him comfortable with where he is in his recovery. It is a lot more work, but we don't want him where he is, and neither does he. I'm focusing on 100 percent, and he's gaining percentage points every week.

Jill needed for people to realize that she wasn't stupid, she was wounded. David has an injury to his brain and this has caused problems with him being able to locate and access "files" in his mind. But he's there, he's smart, and he continues to work at finding ways to access those files. In some cases he is learning new ways to locate the right file, and may in some cases need to create new files. While he might not (yet) be technically competent to handle his own affairs, he's not stupid. He's intelligent, he's sharp, and he needs to be treated as such.

At every point in her recovery, Jill needed to know what she was and wasn't capable of. She needed to know what she could do and what she couldn't. This gave her targets to work toward, problems to solve. If she didn't have a clear concept of what she needed to do, she would flounder. David needs to have short term goals to work toward and accomplish, always with an eye on the path to complete recovery.

All activity, both mental and physical, burns energy. Jill realized very early on that in her situation, if she had been in a traditional rehab facility, with the "energy vampires" that exist there, rather than at home, she would not have been as successful in her recovery. She benefited tremendously by having a mother who was totally dedicated to bringing her daughter back completely. Her mother's goal from the start was 100% recovery for her daughter. Hmmm...

I'm not going to detail the entire book here, but I wanted to mention these few tidbits that I took from this woman's experiences, the connections I found to David's own journey, the journey we are all taking with him.

We're a year and a half along now. Take a look back at some of the early status updates I sent out. We've come a very, very long way. We do have a ways yet to go.

By the way... David is starting to correct people's speech. Also, during sessions where I might ask him a number of questions in order to get him to dig through those brain files of his, he might turn it around and test me with a question, and there'll be a slight smirk on his face.

Tuesday, April 28, 2009
Lately I've been talking to David more and more about climbing Mt. Rainier. I even told him that whenever he sees the mountain that he should tell whoever he is with that he's going to climb that mountain with his dad.

Last week I had him out in the yard with me. He was sitting in his wheelchair watching me work. He suddenly started crying. I hugged him and asked him what was wrong. He tearfully said "I want to help you". After I finished crying, I told him that right now, he has the toughest job in the world, that he's working hard so that he can get out of that chair, and right now my job is to help him. Once that's done, then I'll be glad to have him help me (I told him that since he's retired, he'll have some extra hours on his hands. He smiled at that).

And I told him that once he's out of that chair, we're training to climb the mountain. You know, the usual dad thing I do.

So a couple of days later he and I are finishing up half an hour or so of working on his hands and arms and he looks at me and says "I did a good job". He was getting ahead of my usual "good job, David" and he was smiling as though that was exactly what he was trying to do. He's been doing that lately… He knew what I was going to say and said it first. I can be way too predictable.

So I said something like "you always do a good job, David" and he answered with "training to climb Mt. Rainier". So I hugged him again.

For anyone who's missed the last few updates, be sure to check them out in the archives. There's been some real progress the last few weeks.

Monday, May 18, 2009
David seems to be thinking a little more clearly this past week or so, and may be going thru another of his bursts of progress. His cognition seems sharper, he appears to be more conversational, more interactive. He draws more from his memories as well as from what you say and what is going on around him.

His thoughts often get so far ahead of his ability to speak them that he will stutter and get stuck on a word, which of course really frustrates him. You want to jump in and finish his sentence for him, but trying to make things easier for him wouldn't be helping him in the long run. It's better for his brain recovery to be patient and let him sort it out on his own. Sometimes he'll stop, let out a heavy sigh, and say something like "I will speak more slowly". Sometimes, he'll give up and say something like "I don't remember". When he does, we try to get him back in to try again.

He's not on his feet yet, but I do think it's only a matter of weeks before we have a breakthrough here. The construction people are almost finished with remodeling their house to accommodate David's needs, and once this is out of the way there will be a room that is dedicated to exercise and therapy.

So there's about to be some exercise equipment buying going on. Sem is looking at equipment that David can use now but is also suitable for the entire family. Having his whole family involved is going to be a huge benefit to David's physical recovery and his mental progress as well.

In the meantime, his occupational therapist is putting him in the standing frame and working with him there in addition to the work while in his chair. Ninety-nine percent of his time is spent in his chair, and I know this bothers him. Still, I do see slow advances, though not enough to get him climbing mountains any time soon.

However...

I may have finally gotten the rest of the family a little more excited about that climb. (I've only spent the last year and a half bothering everybody about it.) I know that David is starting to talk about it more and more. Kevin (his son) is planning to make the climb, and he says that he's getting excited about it. We're starting to look at equipment and dates. I'm still targeting next summer, so we're only a year or so out.

Sylvia and I went up to Rainier this past weekend with Kevin and walked one of the easier day hike trails. We wanted to get an idea of what things looked like up there and to start the outdoor hiking part of our training. In addition to the indoor exercising (I have my exercise room and David and Kevin will soon have theirs), we will be taking one of the mountain's day hike trails each month from now to next summer, the hikes being progressively more difficult. This first was at the easy level, (very easy family walk), and was intended to get us acquainted with the area up there and to kick off this part of the training program. By next summer we'll be hiking the expert level trails.

I am hoping that now that Kevin is getting more involved that he will encourage his dad and that they can start to partner up on training.

One final item...

Sylvia and I were sitting and talking with David the other day when he looked at his mom and asked, right out of the blue, "am I getting better?".

The kid is definitely getting better.

Wednesday, May 27, 2009
In the previous update, I said that I believed David might be going thru another of his 'bursts of progress'. I still think so.

Over the past year and a half, he would go through periods lasting weeks with very little outward sign of getting better cognitively. I have to admit that now and then doubt would occasionally creep into my mind. What if what others were saying was true? "This may be as far as it goes, as good as it gets. But we can be thankful that he's alive..."

No. It's not enough.

And then David would suddenly explode with these great progressive leaps, improvements seemingly coming hour by hour, day after day.

That is what's happening now.

It's as though vast areas of his rewiring brain are opening up for business.

A couple of weeks ago, when this latest push began, you could see that he was sharper, to the point where the thoughts were coming faster than he was able to vocalize them. Now, as the advances continue, he is clearly better able to formalize and speak thoughts. It's great stuff. We are all having conversations with him that were impossible just a few weeks ago.

But a key point for me is that I can sense that he is growing up.

During the last nine months or so, as the cognitive improvements brought David back to us more and more, the childlike qualities were very evident. Things would be going well, and then he would say or do something and the realization would jump up out at me: My son is a little boy.

There are those things that he will do or say that can seem wonderful because he is capable of doing them. He couldn't before. Now he can. It tugs at my heart. Yes, he can do that. It's great that he can do that. But my adult son wouldn't do that. My little boy would.

I can't be certain yet, but I'm seeing indications that this might be changing. Perhaps the inhibitions that we develop as we grow up are beginning to wire in. It's not complete yet, but I think it is happening.

In other areas of his cognitive advances, he seems be much sharper in making choices- his own choices. He wants this, he doesn't want that. He wants this flavor, he doesn't want that brand. He's being led less and choosing his own direction more. He is also better able to understand that an action that he takes now moves him toward future goals. He is willing to do things not because he is told to do them but because he understands that it will help him to get better, to get on his feet and to do things for himself.

I remember a number of months ago I said something about wanting one day to be able to sit at the table in our library with David and the rest of the family, to play a game of cards and talk about family stuff. The way we used to.

A lot of things still have to happen to make this come about, but I don't think that day is too far off. We're on the right road and we're moving. We are all of us working to make it happen, and most importantly David is working to make it happen. His most distinctive personality trait, both as a child and as an adult, is that he really, really hates to lose. At anything.

Could be this runs in the family.

Friday, June 05, 2009
When David left for Afghanistan back in early 2007, he stored his car in Kansas, since that was where he flew out

It was delivered to us the other day. Since it will be some time before David is in any position to drive, he and Sem are giving the car to Christy. Besides, though he told me this was the best car he ever had (a Malibu), he says now he wants a Corvette.

So it was dropped off at our house. As it was being unloaded from the back of a flatbed truck, Sylvia started crying and had to go back inside. The last time our boy was in that car, he was healthy and strong and on his way to war.

After it was parked and I had signed all the papers, I sat in the car for a minute. It was easy for me to imagine David driving it into the storage yard, getting it inspected, handing over the keys. He left it just as I was seeing it, fully expecting to pick it up in a year after doing his time in Afghanistan.

How many other parents have watched their child's car, held in storage for months, unloaded from the back of a flatbed truck? There's probably a club somewhere.

David's car was in storage almost two and half years. The Oklahoma plates are long expired. The gas tank is empty, the fuel having evaporated, but someone put in a new battery just before it left Kansas. David says that he wants us to find out who put it in, because we have to pay him for it.

Friday, July 03, 2009
Now that school is out, David and his family are getting out more. They went to Northwest Trek recently, and I heard they were planning to go up to Woodland Park Zoo. They were at Point Defiance earlier.

It isn't quite as easy as just jumping in the car and going, as it would be for the rest of us. David is able to handle things much better than he used to, but you do still need to take into account what the crowds are going to be like, how long the day is going to be, and what David's emotional state is at the time.

And he's still in his wheelchair, so there is that... And there are some personal issues they have to consider.

But he is so far beyond where he was just a few months ago (and when I think of a year and a half ago... oh, man). It's good to see the family getting out and doing family stuff. And it's great to see that David can appreciate the experiences. Sem sends me cell phone pics, and David usually has a big smile on his face (but he's been a photo ham since he was 2 years old).

We're going up to Safeco Field in a few weeks to see a Saturday afternoon baseball game. We'll be in the Terrace Club level, so there'll be smaller crowds, and we'll be able to go through the Terrace Club gate at the sky bridge, so we won't have to deal with the herd mentality at the ground level gates.

I'm hoping to convince Sem to bring David and the family up an hour or two before the game. Not just because the traffic will be lighter, but for me the best part of the trip is often the quiet time pre-game when I can wander around the stadium, watch the teams doing batting practice (Christy caught a foul ball when she was a little girl), and just kicking back and relaxing. I think Sem wants to go to the game and get home. She'll have fun, but she's probably doing this more for David and Kevin (it'll be Kevin's birthday...). She's more of a football (soccer) fan.

Sylvia and I are staying at a nearby hotel this time around so we won't have to deal with the traffic after the game. We'll park the car at the hotel and walk over. Afterward, we'll have dinner at the hotel, wander around Seattle the next morning before coming home. It should be nice. I don't think Sem is comfortable staying at a hotel with David just yet, though. I don't envy them the drive out of the Seattle. Stop and go from the stadium to the freeway, and you're halfway to Tacoma before it thins out.

It's too bad there isn't a later train from Seattle to Olympia. Sylvia and I have taken the train up a few times, but it comes back so early that we have sometimes had to leave the game before it was over in order to get to the station in time. With David in the chair, we'd spend the whole game watching the clock. That wouldn't be much fun.

Friday, July 17, 2009

I don't think David is making the great, progressive cognitive advances that he had been over the last weeks, but is rather beginning to settle onto a new plateau. This was a significant run, and maybe the next one will come along real soon and take us the rest of the way.

We've all commented that over the last weeks it seems as though new areas of his brain are "coming on line".

And he is looking pretty good; he's sharp a lot of the time, but still a ways from being all the way back with us.

David has recently been bringing up memories of the recent past as well as memories from long ago, all on his own. We often talk with him about people and events from the past, and from this he will sometimes draw on memories. But these he's been initiating himself.

Experiences, and our memories of these experiences, are who we are. As David recovers more and more of these, the more I feel I'm seeing his true personality coming through.

Something else I'm noticing is his increasing ability to restrain himself when he grows frustrated or tired. As the day wears on, or when there's just a lot going on, he will sometimes lash out, sometimes quite violently. While this will still happen, I've been seeing him hold back. He'll sit there a little longer than he used to, put up with it a bit longer, before exploding. At least, this seems to be the case.

If this is what is really happening, it could be important. We all get irritable, frustrated, upset. The day wears on, we grow tired, there's too much stuff going on around us, people won't shut up... we blow a circuit...

When this happens with David, we see real quick that he's not yet fully recovered. He can do some serious verbal lashing out, and physically throw a major conniption fit (He may be in a wheelchair, but he is really strong.)

I've watched him closely the last few visits. I've seen him become irritable as he grows tired and uncomfortable. But lately what I see in his expression and his manner is his attempt at restraining himself. If this is really what is going on, it is another part of his brain 'coming on line'. A child throws tantrums. A grown-up isn't allowed to. Okay, granted, David has never been what one would consider a patient person...

On another note... we celebrated Sylvia's birthday the other day. David sang 'Happy Birthday' to his mom. He did a good job. He led the singing. When it came to the part: "happy birthday dear Mom..." David sang "Mommy". But the smile he had on his face was more of a smirk. I'm pretty sure he was just being funny.

And if you think about it, singing *"Happy Birthday dear Mommy"* sounds a little better than *"Happy Birthday dear Mo-om"*. Mostly, though, I think he wanted to be funny.

I'm afraid there's not much physical progress. I really expected that by now he would be lifting himself up with some help, that he would be taking steps using a walker. I have to admit, this worries me. I don't see any reason for him not to be further along. He certainly has the strength and the determination. Something's not clicking in his therapy. I hope it comes soon.

Monday, July 27, 2009
We went up to Safeco Field for a baseball game this past weekend. It was Kevin's birthday and we set this up a couple of months ago. David handled it great and we all had a good time. Well, except for the Mariners. They didn't have a good time.

We went up in the morning and got checked into the Westin (we tried a few months ago to get rooms at the Silver Cloud, across the street from the stadium, for this weekend, but they were already booked). We did have an issue with the rooms at the Westin. Sylvia and I got a really good room on the 29th floor with a fantastic view of the water. Sem had made reservations for a room with a roll-in shower and sleepers for the kids. The room they gave her was smaller than it was supposed to be, no roll-in shower, and the sleeper sofa was like something from fifty years ago (as it turned out, they did have the room they had requested, but it got misplaced in the computer system, so it sat empty waiting for them).

Couple of things... 1) the Westin is further from the stadium than they say. 2) if you go to a baseball game on the same warm, sunny weekend as the Seafair Torchlight Parade and on the same day the Sounders are playing at Quest field, expect crowds. 3) the walk back to the Westin from Safeco Field is all uphill.

We had seats on the Terrace Club level, so once we finally got through the street crowds to the garage elevator up to the sky bridge, it was quieter and we didn't have the crowds we would have had to deal with on the other levels. Terrace Club has 11 to 13 rows in each section. The sections with wheelchair slots in the back row have 11 rows with easy maneuverability. It was really nice. The staff person in our section was very attentive. When he found out that David was a wounded warrior, he went downstairs and the Mariner staff put together a package for him: Felix Hernandez bobble-head, warrior appreciation medallion, T-shirt, stuff like that.

When they presented the colors before the game and sang the National Anthem, David got emotional. His eyes got red and watery. The attendant came over and handed me a tissue. And later, when the attendant brought the package of souvenirs over and we were showing the stuff to David, he started crying again. He was trying to hold it back, but he broke down and said to Sem "I'm emotional".

This was the first time for David and his family at Safeco Field. This was probably a good thing, because for the first eight innings, they at least got to take in the atmosphere of the place and avoid the devastation going on down on the field. And it gave me a chance to explain some of the stuff to them. The ninth inning was pretty exciting, though.

For those of you who may be familiar with the whole Rally Fries sign thing going on, Kevin had made a sign that read "Will Trade Sister for Rally Fries", but he had forgotten it back at the hotel. Too bad.

Once the game was over, the attendant took us to a staff elevator so that we could avoid the elevator at the garage. As we left, he told me that this had been a moving experience for him.

With a pile of souvenirs in David's lap, we trekked back to the hotel, maneuvering our way through baseball, soccer, and Seafair crowds. Back in the lobby, I asked David what he thought of the game.

David said "I had a fun time".

Driving home the next day, I was in the lane where you can veer left to I-90 or stay right on I-5. I got to talking and absentmindedly followed the flow of traffic. Hey, my first time across the I-90 floating bridge...

Friday, August 07, 2009
We had a milestone of sorts this past Wednesday...

We went to the Grays Harbor County Fair. First thing in the morning on the first day of the fair tends to be quieter than waiting for the weekend. I thought it might be easier on David.

But the milestone came in how we got there. His normal mode of travel is to be wheeled up into the van and the wheelchair locked it into place. But on this trip, we transferred David from his wheelchair into the passenger seat of my car. David travelled in a "regular seat", as he called it.

Sem followed behind us in the van. We stopped at the credit union before leaving McCleary, and when David saw Sem walking over to us from the van, he had a big grin on his face. It was a *'hey look at me'*, kind of a grin. It's only seven miles from our house to the fairgrounds, but he had that smile most of the way.

We got to the fairgrounds a little after 10, and spent five hours at the fair. He did very well most of the time, but he was pretty tired near the end and he was getting agitated. It was definitely time to go home.

Oh... David got signed up with the VFW. We were going past their booth, and after talking with us for a minute, they grabbed the application form, got him all signed up, and one of the men slapped a twenty down on the counter and paid the fee.

David gets that reaction a lot.

Tuesday, August 18, 2009
Sylvia and I had David with us this past weekend. For the most part, it was a quiet time, but there were a few things of note.

I was painting one of our outdoor chairs, and David was out on the back deck with me. He watched me for about a minute before saying "I want to help you". So, Sylvia got him a paint brush and we wheeled him up next to the chair. He wasn't able to do much, but he did try to make brush strokes. Once I said "let me get some more paint on that brush for you" and freshened up his paint brush. A few minutes later he said "need more paint."

In the evening, we were watching a not-so-good movie on television. I made occasional comments as to the quality of the production. As the movie ended, David said "weird ending". The reason I bring this up is because I hadn't used the word "weird". A few other adjectives, but not "weird".

We started watching some tv show called "Merlin". I had never watched it before, it looks too much like a teen drama but set in Camelot, but it caught David's attention. And then he started talking. And he went on talking... He had something to say about every character, every scene, and then began on other stuff going on in our lives. After the show was over and we were getting him settled into bed, he was still talking. I understood about half of it.

After we got him settled in, I asked him if he wanted the television on or off. He said "On... or I'll be bored". I went thru the channels with him (fewer of them in that room, cable but no cable box) until we found something he liked. It looked like another weird one. It was either that or Family Guy.

I went back into his room later and asked him if he still wanted the television on. He said "Yes. It's pretty interesting."

Our Chihuahua started barking during the night. David gently called out "Be quiet, Mr. Tuvok."

The next day I was working out in the garden in the front yard off the deck and ramp that I had built for David. We had him sitting in his chair on the deck and he and I talked while I worked. When I would tell him that I was planning on doing one thing or another with the yard, he would say "cost a lot". I would say "I can afford it" or "it wouldn't be that bad". At one point he said "I make good money". I told him that yes, he did. So he asked "do you need some?" I said "Thank you, David, but that's all right. It's your money." He said "what do I need it for?" I said "your house, food, clothes, your kids. Car." And then I remembered he had said before that he wanted a Corvette. So I asked him what kind of car he'd like to buy when he can drive again. He said "Porsche". So I told him he should hang onto his money. He was going to need it.

He enjoys his sister's kids being around. He's usually at our house when he sees them. So over this weekend he asked "Where's Megan and Kimmy?"

And yet... I still find that in one conversation he will seem to be fully with us, almost back to himself, then in the next conversation, he's four years old. One minute everything is fine, and the next he's upset with his mom about nothing.

He knows that I'm "Dad" and that Sylvia is "Mom", but he doesn't know our names.

If you ask him what mountain we're going to climb, he's as likely to say "St. Helens" as "Mt. Rainier".

Physically, I'm only seeing improvement in one area over the past few months. His right wrist seems to be almost 100% normal to me. Very flexible. And his left wrist looks a little better, but he is still a long way from being able to fully straighten or flex it.

I see no indication that he will be standing any time soon, or rolling over or sitting up on his own.

So yes I'm feeling good about his weekend with us, but I'm growing increasingly depressed about the long term. Maybe we need to start focusing attention on just one thing. Maybe we should look at one thing at a time and work on just that, throw everything at it, then move to the next. I don't know...

Friday, August 28, 2009
I'm going to build David a set of parallel bars to help in his walking. He doesn't really have anything right now. He has his standing frame, but that's just a contraption to keep him standing. It lifts him up and holds him in place. It's an important piece of equipment but it serves a very limited purpose.

At this point, he isn't ready for a walker. We can take him by the hands and help lift him from the wheelchair, and he'll stand (sort of) until we ease him back into the chair. That's still a ways from putting his hands on the handles of a walker and asking him to take a step.

He needs an in-between stage that will take him from the standing frame to the walker (and beyond).

I'm hoping this will be the parallel bars. The idea is that every day Sem will wheel him up to one end and pull him to his feet. She can guide him through while one of the kids follows behind, ready with the chair if needed.

If he can make that dozen steps through the bars every day, then before long he should be able to transition to a walker and then move freely about the house. After that, walks outside, then trails, then...

I've noticed that David is very good at performing those tasks that he is required to do with Sem on a regular basis, such as his transition from bed to wheelchair and the other way around. If he uses the parallel bars every day, or twice a day, then he'll get just as good at actually taking steps. He's strong enough, and he's determined. He has the desire.

He's growing increasingly frustrated with his situation. He really, really doesn't like it.

So I'm off to Home Depot.

Friday, September 04, 2009
Sylvia spent most of this past Wednesday with David and Sem, and she came away at the end of the day feeling pretty good.

For one thing, he knew who she was. All too often when asked who she is he will say "I don't know". On this day, it was "that's my Mom". I don't think he doesn't know, but rather he lost the word "mom" when matching it to the person.

Also, at one point during the day he said to her "you used to call me Bo-Boy". When she said "Yes, that's right", he responded "I like that".

Sounds like there are more connections happening in that brain of his.

He's very interested in the parallel bars we're building for him. I believe he's making the connection between this piece of equipment and getting out of the wheelchair and onto his feet. As I indicated in the last update, he is increasingly aware of his current situation and doesn't like it.

While he does have the drive, I still think he needs to be pushed more. He understands what's going on and that an action leads to a consequence. He needs to see the reward for his effort and that it doesn't have to always be like this. But we also need to provide him with the tools he needs, whether it's parallel bars or short term goals so that he can realize accomplishments. Like any of us, successes can lead to more successes.

Tuesday, September 08, 2009
We still need to do a little work on David's parallel bars that
we've put together, but it's completed enough that we were able
to have him give it a try.

One thing became very clear, very quickly.

We don't want to have someone standing directly in front of
David to help keep him up and attempt to guide him along, and
especially not with a "gait belt" to support him. He was hunched
over and basically sitting in the gait belt with his face in Sem's
shoulder the entire time. As excited as he was to give the parallel
bars a try, It was sad and I'm sure he was dIsappoInted.

So once we had an hour or so away from it, I wanted to give it
another go, but handled differently, so that everyone would
come away with a better experience.

This time no one was inside the bars. We stood to either side.
Also, we didn't push him to walk this time around. We wanted
him to use the bars as support to stand, and to do it all on his
own.

Sem wheeled the chair to the end of the bars and brought it in
just a little. We asked David to hold onto the bars and pull
himself up, though he didn't really need any encouragement. He
put a hand on either bar and pulled himself out of the chair. He
didn't stand completely straight, but it wasn't bad at all. While
his back wasn't fully straight, he wasn't hunched over. And more
importantly, no one helped, other than to stand ready if needed.
He did it on his own.

David stayed on his feet for five or ten seconds, then eased
himself back into the chair. After half a minute or so, he pulled
himself up again. Again, after a few seconds, he sat back down.
He went through this exercise half a dozen times.

Sem then got a bar and laid it across the parallel bars out in front
of David. She and I held tight to the bar and had David reach out
in front of him and hold onto the cross bar. Using this, over the
next five or ten minutes, he pulled himself up another half a
dozen times .

We didn't try to have him walk this time. Being able to pull himself up to his feet on his own was enough of a milestone. And he was quick to do it without prompting from us. I think that with the path down the parallel bars clear and visible to him, where David can see the goal of the end of the bars, that at some point, as he is standing there all on his own, he will take the first step.

Friday, September 18, 2009
Sylvia and I went over to David and Sem's house this past Sunday and watched the Seahawks game. It was a fun game and we had a good time. I would have liked to have seen David a little more active, though. Even at the most exciting plays, there wasn't much of what you would call participation. He watched it, seemed interested, but he appeared rather passive. I'm hoping for more. Of everyone in the family, he's the biggest football fan.

At one point I asked him about a long retired football player. "David, what was the name of that Bronco quarterback that always gave us such trouble?" David quickly came back with "John Elway". David will remember that, but half the time when I ask him which mountain we're going to climb, he'll say St. Helens rather than Rainier.

We also did a little more work on the parallel bars that we made for him, and during half time wheeled him over and had him do his standing exercises. He was ready to go. Once in position, he held onto the bars and stood, held for five seconds and sat back down, repeated this a number of times. He brings himself up just fine, but we often had to encourage him to stand straight. Even at that, he's not fully straight, but he is getting better. I also had to work with him to get him to put his feet flat on the floor. Not quite there yet, either.

I think with daily repetitions at the bars, he'll be standing on his own soon. Not just at the parallel bars, but with any support. I also believe that it shouldn't be too long and he will take a step on his own when standing at one end of the parallel bars and looking at the other end. It'll just take working at the equipment every day. He seems eager and looks at me expectantly when he's standing, as if to say 'okay, I'm ready now, let's do this'.

David is coming to stay at our house this Sunday-Monday. He and I will watch another Seahawks game. We're playing the 49ers, his grandpa's team. Sylvia's dad said he really wishes he could be up here to watch it with us. Hey, it's only a few hours by plane. I'll supply the beer, Robert can supply the losing team (I hope I don't have to change this update on Monday).

Tuesday, September 22, 2009
David stayed with us this past Sunday and Monday and had a really good time. He was in very good humor, laughed and smiled a lot, and seemed really sharp.

He and I spent a little too much time watching television, but at least we talked a lot about what we were watching. Yes, I know the Seahawks lost. They looked pretty bad, and we talked about that. At one point I commented that we had finally managed to stop Gore from punching through our defensive line and running for a touchdown, and David said "first time for everything".

We did come up with a standing exercise, and we worked on it five or six times over the two days. I held a bar out in front of him and above him, and David had to place his hands on it, grip it, and pull himself out of his wheelchair and to his feet. I did have to do some pulling in order to maintain position, but David had to actually pull himself up and hold himself in position, all on his own. He did very well. Sylvia took a couple of pictures. I'll see about putting them on to the website this weekend.

Repetition, repetition, repetition. Whether holding a bar out in front of him, or positioning him at one end of the parallel bars, it sure seems that having David pull himself to his feet on his own, and encouraging him to do it properly, helps. And it's really good for his morale, and he likes doing it.

Sylvia heard David moving about in his bed on Sunday night and she went in to make sure that he was all right. She said that he was shifting about as if to move onto his side. After almost two years of laying flat on his back, we're seeing more and more indications that he will soon be able to roll onto his side on his own. Maybe some exercises here as well. Once he can consistently roll onto his side, it shouldn't be long before he can push himself up into a sitting position. At one point his physical therapist was doing something along these lines.

Okay, beyond the jokes about some of the television that we were watching, I did get some real laughs out of David on Monday.

We have a pool in our back yard, encircled with a deck. This summer we built a ramp to get David up onto the pool deck. Now, the water has recently started to turn rather cold, but I wasn't ready to give up swimming for the summer. So I bought a wetsuit.

On Monday I gave the suit a test run. We wheeled David up onto the deck, and I went into the pool shack and changed. When I stepped out and David saw me, he got the biggest grin. He thought his dad in a wetsuit walking around on the pool deck was really funny. And he started laughing, especially when I went into the water. But hey, the suit works. I can keep swimming.

Wednesday, October 07, 2009
We had a family gathering the other day for my birthday. There were a few people there who hadn't seen Little David in quite a while. They were really surprised at how much better he looked than the last time. Reading about progress in a status update just isn't the same as seeing it in person.

There is one bit of bad news. David went in for Botox shots on Tuesday. Remember, he gets these a few times a year to help limber up his constricted muscles. At this last session, Sem and David were told that the constriction of his left wrist was permanent. The Botox injections weren't going to do any good.

When we were in Palo Alto, the top doctor there had discussed surgery for that wrist with another doctor that specialized in the field. At that time, it was decided to wait and see whether we could get any improvement through less invasive means. Well, I guess I need to start pursuing this other option. It involves going in and cutting the constricted muscle strands, so I don't imagine that it would happen until his inability to fully use that hand becomes more of an issue in his recovery.

I'm still hoping we can do more with one of his feet without going to such extremes. When standing, David has a very hard time putting both feet flat on the floor. One heel is always raised. We need to work at having David use that foot, and to make a conscious effort to push that heel down and limber up those muscles whenever standing.

Sylvia and I have been going up to Mt. Rainier to hike some of the lower trails, in preparation of the climb. Doing these hikes on the mountain gave me some sense that I was drawing nearer my ultimate goal.

But now I want to become more aggressive in my hikes and do them more often. I need something closer. We found some great hiking trails over at Ellis Cove in Olympia. Some of them are steep enough to give you a workout if you push it, and it's only half an hour from my house. I'm going to start going there every weekend, and I'm going to drag Kevin (David's son) along with me as often as he'll come. He still wants to make the climb with us.

Well... an anniversary coming up. October 12th is just around the corner. On this date two years ago, I got the phone call.

Tuesday, October 27, 2009
We haven't been able to see much of David the last couple of weeks, but Sylvia does talk to him on the phone almost every day. He likes to talk to his mom, even if it's only to say hi.

Things have been kind of quiet, not much in the way of progress or breakthroughs, but there are two items I want to let you know about that could lead to something.

David's portable wheelchair finally arrived. This is one of those chairs that you can collapse and toss into the trunk of a car. One of the main reasons for getting this was to make it easier to transport David around in a vehicle other than the customized van. Currently David gets wheeled up the ramp and his chair is locked into position in the passenger location.

But his current wheelchair is such a beast that it's difficult to store it in the back of most cars, making it impractical to take him anywhere in any car other than their van. Now, though, we can help him into the passenger seat of another car and put the portable chair in the back or in the trunk. This means that when he comes to stay with us for a weekend, we aren't stuck at home. I can take him fishing (yes!) or we can just go out for a drive if we want. I think that from now on we're going to be spending a lot of time out on the road whenever he comes to visit.

And one big side benefit of this chair that I hadn't thought of (but should have)... Sem told us that when she helped David move from his regular chair to the new chair for the first time that he started using his feet to move around the living room. He can't do that with his regular wheelchair, even with the footrest attachments removed, as the chair sits too high for his feet to touch the ground.

I'm hoping that the more mobile he becomes, the more he will want to be mobile, and will strive to work harder at being independent. If he can move around the house on his own, maybe he will work at reaching out with his hands and trying to pick things up when he gets to where he's going. If he's using his feet to move around the house, maybe he'll make a conscious effort to use his hands to maneuver the chair around as well. Who knows?

And the second item that I wanted to mention... David went to the dentist a while back to prep for his new teeth. Well, his inserts are ready and he goes in this Friday. I think this will help him psychologically (those front teeth have been missing for two years now). Having his front teeth back should also make it easier for him to talk more clearly, so we should start seeing more improvement here as well.

I'll send out another update as soon as David gets his new front teeth.

Saturday, October 31, 2009

David didn't get his teeth yesterday. There's still another step or two. The "roots" were put in a couple of months ago, but I guess they hadn't made the impressions for the implants yet.

Okay... I've come to an important decision regarding the climb up Mt. Rainier.

I believe that David could have been ready this coming summer, but for a number of reasons I don't think he will be. I'm pretty sure that he'll be ready come the following summer (2011), but I have my doubts about the 2010 season.

However, I still plan to make the climb this year.

To start putting it off with "maybe next year" would be a mistake. Once I start pushing it out to "next year" and "next year", it'll never happen. He'll never go. So I'm going. If David isn't ready, well, then I'll make this one a recon climb. David, I'll let you know how it goes.

I've said it before. David is the most competitive person I've ever known; even more so than me. I'm going to involve him in every stage of the preparations. He knows how much I want him to make this climb. Hell, everyone does by now.

We need to work with him every day, get him on his feet, get him moving one foot in front of the other, and then walking. Give him a target to work towards. But if come next summer he isn't ready, then he isn't ready. That's only half a year away, so even if he's walking, there's a matter of strength, coordination and endurance.

I wanted my very first climb up the mountain to be with my son. I don't think that's going to happen now, and that really, really hurts. I get an ache in my chest just writing the words. But I don't think I have a choice. If I put it off because he isn't ready, then I have no doubt it will be put off again, and then again.

If I have to make this first climb alone, the climb that we planned for these last two years, I'm hoping it will set the stage for a father/son climb in 2011. If not, then I'll make a second climb

alone, and then a third climb alone in 2012, and every year after
that until Little David comes with me.

He's not the only stubborn one in the family.

I contacted Rainier Mountaineering in mid November of 2009
about signing up with one of their scheduled climbs for the next
summer. I found that they won't hold a spot for you until you put
$300 down, and then you have to provide the rest at least 90
days ahead of the climb date.

I was looking at one of the climbs scheduled for the end of
July. The woman on the phone told me there were still spots
available on that team, but that most of the climbs scheduled for
July and August usually fill up sometime in December, and all
their climbs are usually full by the end of February.

I wasn't quite ready to put down the requisite $300, so I
decided to wait. When I checked back a few weeks later, right at
the end of November, I saw that my climb date had filled. I
quickly chose another, July 23-26, and put my money down.

So I was going. I knew by that time that I was going to be
making this first climb without David. It would be on his behalf,
but nonetheless the thought of going without him was
heartbreaking. I had set a crazy goal two years earlier that my son
and I would climb Mt. Rainier together. Back then when I made
that insane pronouncement, David was about an hour behind us
in a Medivac cargo jet, flying across the country in a vegetative
state and his body broken a dozen different ways and only just
starting to heal. None of that mattered. Hell no. He and I were
going to climb a mountain.

Now, as the date drew nearer, I knew that he wasn't anywhere
near ready. But he had come so damn far; much farther than any
of the doctors and specialists had believed. We had been told to
"be thankful for what you have", that "this is probably all that
you're going to get". At one point we had been directed to a
"facility" that specialized in "housing patients such as your son".

We had refused to accept any of that. David, a son and a
husband and a father and a brother, was going to get better.

Okay, I had to accept the fact that he wasn't going to be ready
to make the climb this year. But I was afraid that if I said "that's
okay, David. Maybe we'll make the climb next year" that I would

be making that same statement every year, and the climb would never happen. David would never walk.

So I resolved that *this year* I would make the climb alone, on his behalf. This year. But I would involve him as much as possible in all the preparations, all the training that I would have to go through leading up to July. And come July, David and his family would stay at Paradise Lodge at the foot of the mountain. I would stand before him, let him know that I was making the climb for him this year, and that he and I had a lot of work to do if he was going to be ready for the next climb, and then I would set off.

I believed that the preparations leading up to the climb would help motivate him, that he and I would work all the harder to get him out of that chair and walking. At least I hoped so.

I will make this first climb without my son. Come next year, if he's not ready, I will again make the climb alone, on his behalf. And the next year, and the year after that, and every year until he makes the climb with me.

Update...

As of this writing Little David is still in the wheelchair, still unable to stand on his own, much less walk. Perhaps one day, but for now, I'll be making the Mt. Rainier ascent in his name.

There have been a number of setbacks, but we're hopeful the climb will happen next July. This past summer Little David's son Kevin began hiking with me, and the plan is for us to summit the mountain together.

David continues to improve cognitively. Progress is slow, but it is there nonetheless. I am frequently surprised at observations he'll make, statements he'll blurt out. He's definitely not fully back, and I don't know how far he'll go, but as I always say, I'm going for 100%. Why would I ever put a limit on it?

David R. Beshears
October 2014